Give Yourself Permission to

LIVE A BIG LIFE ™

CEO & Founder
Joan Burge
Speaks to Women

For information about special discounts for bulk purchases,
please call 1-855-315-LIVE or write
Live a Big Life, Attn: Order Department,
2766 Evening Rock St., Las Vegas, NV 89135

www.JoanBurgeBIGLife.com

ISBN: 978-0-9717456-8-1

What Everyday Women Are Saying
About Live a BIG Life

"Throughout her memoir, Joan Burge offers colorful – sometimes emotional – examples of self-empowerment from her personal and professional life. This is a must read for any woman who needs inspiration to move forward, to reach her potential, and to persevere. Upon reading Give Yourself Permission to Live a BIG Life you will understand the need for having the five pillars and the passion to love yourself, live life, and "Live BIG." And last, but not least, RLP ... Red Lipstick Power!" –Denise Holota

"Live a BIG Life –truly touched me. Sharing her own poignant story, Joan carried me along with her on her life's journey. I found the quotes throughout each chapter giving me an inner strength at a time in my life when I truly need it. We are all on our own personal life's journey and after reading her story, I too want to Live a BIG Life. These will be my words to live by and this book showed me the way." –Debbie Gross

"It's a memoir, a self-help book, and an inspirational book all in one. Every woman of every age and of every stature should read this book – not just once but regularly and often. Not only is there so much to learn, but there are so many basic yet valuable reminders that we, as everyday women, need to be reminded of. As we check things off of our calendars living our days, we think we are living a big life, but after Joan unveils a new definition of BIG, we will realize that we are living a busy life, not a BIG life. Joan will tell us and remind us that we can live a BIG life." –Geri Tomich

"What an amazing story! I have known Joan since 2006 and she continues to inspire me each time our paths cross. Her love for LIFE is an inspiration to all women and a testimony to the person that she is today. Joan leaves a positive and lasting impact on all women as we continue through our BIG Life reaching for the stars to fulfill our potential. I feel blessed to have Joan in my life." –Cathy Baker

What Everyday Women Are Saying About Live a BIG Life

"Live a BIG Life ... has a BIG meaning behind it! This book spoke to me on many different levels, as an administrative professional, a wife, a mother and a friend. It truly makes you think about the "pillars" in your own life, and how you need to strengthen them every day, so they never come crumbling down around you. As Joan writes about that memorable 1999 Annual Conference, I'm proud to have met her that day, as I left feeling so empowered after surviving that experience. Floyd didn't stand a chance against the Red Lipstick Power!" –Sherry Viering

"I found this book to be an inspirational guide to women's empowerment, no matter what position they may hold. However, what sets this book apart, is the lifelong journey the real experiences with the author's own personal account of how she attained her personal "BIG life." It teaches and guides women how to handle situations they may normally find intimidating. By teaching them how to look at circumstances with a different outlook, enabling them to face challenges with their red lipstick, this book guides women on their journey to control their lives and claim their rights." –Danielle Strong

"This was a very inspirational book to read! I could not put it down. I read 97 pages in one day. There are many emotional parts that made me tear up! There are a lot of Life Changing lessons in BIG. This was an easy book to read and I really enjoyed it!" –Julie Friedman

"I definitely dug out my bright red lipstick to wear! Especially in this down economy, it's nice to have that "pep talk" and be able to see someone else's success story to really give hope." –Julia Paajanen

Tell Me About Your BIG Life

Every woman has a story. What's yours? What obstacles or hardships have you overcome? How did you muster up courage? What unique event has shaped you and made you a better or stronger woman? What was the most difficult thing you have ever done? What was the bravest action you have taken?

I have been surrounded by women all my life. However, since 1990 when I started my training and professional speaking career, I have been blessed to be in the presence of thousands of women. They have shared very personal stories with me. I have seen women overcome financial hardship, fight cancer, assist their ailing husband or parents, support their adult children, work long hours and struggle through a job loss. The common thread in all this is that we are not alone. Women are strong, adaptable, flexible and can laugh together.

I believe that if we open our hearts and listen, we can learn a great deal from others. We do not have to go through the "tough stuff" alone. And when we talk about our heartaches or challenges, we give permission for other women to share their stories, which creates an amazing bond. We lift each other up when we share.

I would love to hear from you. I am accepting short stories for consideration to post on www.JoanBurgeBIGLife.com, a web site for women.

Please keep your story to 750 words or less and submit it to:

MyStory@JoanBurgeBIGLife.com

Whether we post your story or not, in appreciation for sharing your story with me, I will send you my audio CD, *Juggling Work, Home and Your Personal Life*.

Thank you!
Joan Burge
Author

Also by Joan Burge

Books
Who Took My Pen ... Again?
Underneath It All
Become an Inner Circle Assistant
Real World Communication Strategies That Work
The Survival Guide for Secretaries and Administrative Assistants
A Survival Guide for the Novice Entrepreneur
Remarkable Women

E-zine and Blogs
Monday Motivators™
600+ Blogs at OfficeDynamics.com

Audios
Gain Recognitions and Achieve Your Worth
Goal Setting: Tactics to Advance Your Career
Juggling Work, Home and Your Personal Life
Success Is 90% Attitude
World Class Assistant™

Training Manuals
Be a Star Achiever™
Star Achieving Attitudes™
Building a Star Partnership™
Reaching Stardom™
Give a Stellar Performance™
Be a Shining Star™
Expanding the Star Team™
The Contemporary Star Performer™
Star-Achieving Attitudes™
Be a Stellar Ambassador™
Coaching a Star Team™
Mastering a Stellar Career™
World Class Assistant™ Parts 1 and 2

Dedication

To Dave, the Love of My Life
You have always been a BIG part of my life.
Thank you for the amazing adventure. I would not have moved
away from Cleveland, grown and spread my wings if it was
not for your great love and support. Thank you for
being my internal consultant and personal shopper!
I miss your touch, but we will always be connected in spirit.

To Lauren, Our First Born
Thank you for your amazing strength through your
dad's illness and the tremendous support
you have given me the past several years.
You have grown into a strong and
bright young woman. I am so proud of you.

To Brian, Our Wild Child
You always gave me a run for my money
because you were such an inquisitive child.
While you could not be around much when your dad was ill,
you have shown up at just the right time for me
as I venture into my new life.

To Wade, Who Has Always Been Like a Son
Since you were two years old, you have been a
loving, caring and giving person.
Thank you for spending six weeks at my home in 2010
to nurse your dad and be my rock.

To Jeff, My Son-in-Law
Thank you for all the wonderful dinners you cooked,
organizing your dad's meds for me,
being level-headed and loving.
Dad loved watching football with you!

Bradley, Madison, Eian and Ethan
My loving grandchildren who mean the world to me.
You kept me laughing when I wanted to cry!
You made me smile when my heart was breaking inside.
You kept me company when I felt so lonely.
You light up the darkest room, and I love you so much!

May all of you Live a BIG Life!

Acknowledgements

I have been blessed to have so many people come into my life. I have been blessed to be able to spread my teachings and philosophies to thousands of administrative professionals and other career professionals since 1990. It is a privilege and an honor to touch so many lives, and I am humbled by the assistants who follow me from around the world, both online and who travel to Las Vegas to attend my workshops and conferences.

I want to acknowledge all the people who crossed my path during my life. I cannot possibly list all the wonderful men and women who inspired, taught and uplifted me. I learned as much from you as you have learned from me. I opened my mind and learned that my way is *not* the only way, that my way is *not* the only *right* way and that I have been able to Live a BIG Life because of the thousands of individuals who passed me on my journey. Some of you popped into my life at just the right time for a special reason; others have been in my life forever, even though we don't talk very often. Many of you are held close in my thoughts and prayers.

I want to give recognition to my mother, Santina (Adorney) DeGirolamo, my father, Anthony DeGirolamo, and my grandparents who came to the United States from Sicily and Fogia, Italy. You have always been the greatest parents a child could ask for; both of you were a pillar of strength in times of adversity and full of love, joy and generosity. I always said I came from good stock—the DeGirolamo family and the Adorney family.

I am grateful for my sisters, stepmom, cousins, nieces, nephews, brothers-in-law and sisters-in-law. I am blessed to have such a big, close-knit family. Thanks for being a part of my life in good times and in bad.

A huge thank you to my incredible *angels* at Office Dynamics: Jasmine Freeman and Michele Busch. As I scurry around like a crazy woman short on time, you keep everything afloat with calm, big smiles and great attitudes. You make me laugh and keep me young.

I could never have managed all the chaos of the past five years if it weren't for my Las Vegas family consisting of wonderful neighbors, church family, business colleagues and good friends. May we have many more good years together.

My across-the-street neighbor, Sharyn, has been a pillar of strength and also makes me laugh often. Sharyn was a caregiver for 14 years to her husband, Dave, who passed in 2007. Sharyn is a great listener and up to new adventures with me! She is known as 'Aunt Sharyn' to my grandchildren.

John and Ruth Ahlbrand deserve a special note of thanks. John sold us our beautiful home when we moved to Las Vegas; I immediately rented office space from them when we moved here; they offered Dave a career opportunity in real estate, moved to our neighborhood and became our best friends. The four of us had many good times. Thanks for the memories!

Thank you, Marilyn, for coaching me through this book and being a friend. We have worked on some interesting projects together, and I look forward to more of them!

An Auspicious Beginning

Just prior to my arrival into the world, the obstetrician told my dad that the umbilical cord was wrapped around my neck. "You must choose. Should I save your wife or your baby?" My dad answered, "My wife." My dad went to church and prayed and prayed. We both lived!

I am enormously grateful to be alive.

Table of Contents

Introduction

CHAPTERS

Table of Contents
(continued)

Introduction

I'm blessed to **Live a BIG Life**. I set goals and know I'll achieve them and then set new goals. It's a wonderful way to live life! I've always been an action-oriented person. At age seven, I was out selling my mother's already-read magazines to neighbors. I was always strong and strong-willed. And enthusiasm for life and action just kept bubbling up inside of me. Now the time for me to write this book had come. I couldn't have done it sooner, and I'm about to share with you why this is true and why I wrote this book.

I took secretarial courses in high school and devoured them with a passion. I knew exactly what I wanted to do after graduation. For the next twenty years, I worked as a secretary. My husband, Dave, and I lived in eight different states as his career blossomed. Each time we moved, I knew I could get a good job, and I did. During those years, I worked in twelve different companies. I learned something of value from each accomplished executive I supported.

After twenty years of work as an administrative assistant, I was ready for something different. I loved my career and was appreciated by the executives I supported, so it wasn't surprising that I wanted to find a way to help others excel in this profession too. I developed and wrote four training manuals, honed my speaking and presentation skills, consulted with an excellent mentor and founded a new company, Office Dynamics, Ltd.

The next twenty years were spent traveling to many states to conduct workshops and train administrative assistants to be the best they could be. My teachings blossomed from a core philosophy called Star Achievement. This philosophy spotlights an assistant's potential to be a *star-performing* administrative professional. All it takes is the right combination of *skill, attitude, teamwork* and *strategy*. The focus is on acknowledging and enhancing the qualities and attributes we already have within us and then developing new skills and techniques. From this philosophy I created a rich, in-depth curriculum called the Star Achievement Series® featuring beliefs and concepts that ultimately saved me and thousands of administrative professionals over and over again in work and personal life. The Star Achievement philosophy is about changing behaviors and attitudes over time. It's about evolution and therefore never ends. It *says* to each person, "As good as you are today, you have the potential to do more. Dig deeper, find the special gifts you were blessed with and bring those forth into your work and the world." *Star Achievement is a way of thinking ... being ... and performing.* It becomes a way of life, and once a person embraces this philosophy, she (or he) applies it to everything she embraces (e.g., job, personal relationships) for the rest of her life. It's very powerful and has enriched the lives of thousands of people.

I worked with employers too, helping to strengthen assistant/executive communication channels. Results were almost 100 percent positive, and I was called back to help employees reinforce skills or to introduce methods to employees in other departments. Clients frequently told executives in other companies about my services, and they hired me too. Although my fledgling business experienced some ups and downs, it didn't take long to realize that the Office Dynamics business model worked. It was unique—a first of its kind. The four Star Achievement Series® Training Manuals I wrote and used in the early days were followed by others. Today there are a total of twelve workbooks, all of which are up-to-the-minute and in step with our times. There are Office Dynamics' conferences, annual conventions, workshops, full-length books, blogs, e-zines and other Internet communications customized to serve this population. On February 9, 2012, Office Dynamics Ltd. officially became Office Dynamics International. We have followers around the world, and women come from Russia, Italy, Qatar and France to attend our world-renowned annual conference and high-end administrative boot camps in Las Vegas.

Don't assume, however, that everything has been honey and roses all these years. I have battled through devastating personal tragedies too.

It's time to share what I've learned from these experiences and from the great numbers of women who have attended Office Dynamics workshops and conferences. It's time to pen my memoirs, not because I'm a celebrity, but because I'm an ordinary but very determined woman who feels the force of something far greater than I am prodding me to write this book. I write about many things, including my spirituality, and I don't worry about admonitions that it's not smart to talk about it. I would not be where I am today if it weren't for God's Grace. I'm "talking" about everything I can think to tell you that *inspires you to Live a BIG Life too*. The rewards are like no other earthly rewards. You have only to recognize this can be yours. And then you have to let it happen!

The **Live a BIG Life** *story* is for all women ... some may be doctors, nurses, teachers, accountants, engineers, pilots, retail sales people, retirees and stay-at-home moms. Others may be writers, architects, policewomen, fire fighters, airline attendants, actresses, dancers, waitresses and artists, caretakers and judges. I want to reach as many women as possible. Each person is a *work-in-progress* unless she willingly halts her own progress. After twenty years of speaking to dedicated women who hold administrative or executive assistant positions in offices and learning from them, after coming through my early years with a mom who outsiders dubbed "crazy" and after recently riding a long-term emotional roller coaster while my husband and life partner battled against pancreatic cancer and finally succumbed to this monster, I am now feeling like a veritable volcano ready to erupt!

This book contains intimate details and graphic word pictures and may be better suited to the sensibilities of a thirty-something woman. Pancreatic cancer is a foul foe, and I write copiously about my husband's three and one-half years battle with it and what it was like to be his round-the-clock caregiver during the final months of his life. When

xvi   Give Yourself Permission To Live A BIG Life

Dave died, I lost my business partner, lover, advisor, personal shopper (Dave loved to buy my clothes and made excellent selections) and best friend. He was my rock!

I'm just an ordinary woman, not a celebrity, but my husband's courage deserves a spotlight just the same. He lost his war, but I survived this horrendous and (seemingly) un-ending ordeal and pray you may never have a loved one who must battle pancreatic cancer. We know life brings many seasons to our doors. Even when life appears to be practically perfect, we know there are DESERT IN-BETWEEN years, times (between the practically perfect times) that are bleak, and when everything you do requires enormous effort. I attended a series of lectures at my church that were entitled DESERT IN-BETWEEN, and I use these words on occasion since they're so descriptive. No one's life is simply a series of fun and games. Need I remind anyone that each year thousands of children are diagnosed with Autism? Multitudes of seniors are afflicted with dementia or Alzheimer's? Staggering numbers of service men and women return home from wars missing limbs or suffering from brain injuries? People who we love die, and we must persevere without them. Some say, "Necessity is the mother of invention." I say that you must be prepared well in advance of "necessity," and the beauty of this recommendation is that it can be done. You will emerge on the other side of a major challenge knowing full well you did your without-a-doubt, without-cause-for-recrimination, without question—personal best.

I have been training administrative professionals, especially women (only 3 percent of the people in this profession are males) to be the very best they can be in corporate America: **I had been *them* for twenty years!** Mine is practical information about how to be a woman in this world.

As my 60th birthday appears on the horizon, I find myself vibrant and alive and thriving, but I have held hands with *death*. When Dave first passed, I told the hospice counselor I felt like there was a heavy chain around my ankle. At the same time, I was provoked by my dreams and aspirations and I envisioned *bursting open*. I felt guilty since Dave had only just died a few weeks earlier. I didn't have to worry because I didn't *burst open* until one year later. Finally, I am at peace, feel free and know joy. I had forgotten who the real Joan DeGirolamo Burge is, and I was so happy to meet her again. She is even stronger, smarter, more empathetic, and more loving than ever before. Of course I miss Dave intensely, but the weight of this loss no longer suffocates me. I am okay! Come along with me now and examine what it's like to Live a BIG Life and make the small but mighty adjustments so you can do it too.

////////

Chapter One

Just Before My Princess Wedding ... OMG!

"In three words I can sum up everything
I've learned about life. It goes on."
—ROBERT FROST

I was baptized and raised in a Catholic Italian family and from grades one through twelve attended Catholic schools. When it was time for high school I was enrolled in Notre Dame, a Catholic high school for girls only. At that time, the Catholic Church was so strict that you didn't dare walk into any other church or you would burn in hell. That's what I was raised to believe. The Catholic Church was the one true church, and we would go to church every Sunday. The Catholic religion was highly revered by my family. So, when it was time to marry Nick, my teenage sweetheart, we married in the Catholic Church.

We had a fairy-tale wedding with a large wedding party, tents in the back yard, beautiful flowers everywhere, champagne flowing and food fit for royalty. The female guests wore long, elegant movie-star-like gowns, and the men were in formal attire. It was a huge Italian Catholic wedding, and my dad spared no expense. He rolled out the red carpet for me from morning until evening. My gown was spectacular. We bought it in New York on a special trip my parents took me on several months before our wedding date. My dad really surprised me when he arranged for Nick to fly to New York as well. We sipped champagne, and Nick bought my wedding ring in New York. I thought life was just absolutely wonderful!

And then, one day just weeks before my lavish wedding, we came home to find my mother excitedly scurrying around the house telling us that the Pope was coming to visit and she had to get everything ready. My dad and I were bewildered. What was happening? Where did this come from? She wanted to set our dining room table with fine china and her beautiful stemware, but we didn't know what to do. She was saying things that were bizarre and made no sense. I was so scared because the mother I knew was rational and put-together. This new woman, who had come out of nowhere, was nothing like that.

Finally, we decided to invite our extended family to our house. We sat in the large living room together and basically stared at one another, dumbfounded. We didn't know what to think, what to say and what to feel. We were distraught with worry about her and these new delusions.

After consulting with my dad's friend who was a medical specialist, my dad finally admitted her into an institution for treatment. I was with my dad the first time we had to admit her, and it was heartbreaking to say the least. She went from a beautiful, big home to a cold, barren hospital room. My mother was always ladylike and proper: she had manicured nails, dressed meticulously and always had her hair done and makeup on. Now she was in an old hospital gown.

My mother was diagnosed with severe manic depression. You might be thinking, "Isn't all manic depression the same?" No, it is not. There are various levels on a continuum that goes from extreme high to extreme low. In years to come, she would try to commit suicide more than once, receive shock therapy, be locked in sterile rooms, have unpredictable mood swings and be in and out of hospitals. Each time, it was painful for us to watch. At the age of nineteen, I had lost the mother I had known as a little girl and, in time, accepted her new path and loved her unconditionally.

Under sedation, my mother was able to be at my *Princess Wedding*, and everything went off without a hitch.

Today we recognize manic depression as a bipolar problem. There are medicines available that enable people with this chemical imbalance to live relatively normal lives. But for almost twenty years, my dad had to contend with my mother's severe manic depression, which wasn't understood or properly treated. My dad, who ran his own business, would have to abruptly leave his office or a customer's house to go home to take care of her or get someone else to be with her. My mother's illness destroyed my dad for many years. His business and his relationships with friends and family all suffered. People looking from the outside saw a big house with gardens and Cadillacs in the driveway. They saw a family who took

vacations and appeared to have everything, but they didn't see the trag-
edy and couldn't know of the heartache and pain.

When my mom was going through upbeat periods, she was very
good to my sisters and me. Janet was the first born, and then I came
along five years later. Ten years after me, Gina was born. Our mom
would urge us to embrace life with all its joys, hurts and sorrows. "When
you're happy, really be happy. Be joyous. When you hurt, embrace the
pain. Don't be afraid to hurt." That always resonated with me, and she
set a perfect example. She taught me to look at a situation and think,
"Oh my I don't like how I feel; I'm feeling so uncomfortable," or, "I
don't understand this," or, "We've had an illness in our family," or, "My
husband just lost his job and it's killing me," and respond by knowing it's
okay to feel it, embrace it and say, "Okay, *bring it on.* I've got this change
coming at me, but I view it as *waves of change that come over us* but don't
knock us down. We're still standing." She wanted us to seize the day
and especially not let the best times pass without notice or appreciation.

I'll never forget her good words of advice when I was seventeen and
dating a boy named Jerry. I thought he adored me until I discovered that
he was secretly dating another girl too. That afternoon my mother found
me sobbing in my bedroom; the window shades were down, and *I was
a mess.* Mom told me to stop sitting there feeling *sorry for me.* "Let the
sun shine in and wash your face. Every time you go through something
difficult, God is teaching you a lesson." *Actions speak louder than words.
Remember this next time you meet a boy who shows interest in you.* Mom
tried to help me put a positive spin on the experience.

My mom would be thrilled to see this book! She loved to write.
She wrote and wrote after she was diagnosed with manic depression.
Much of her writing was bizarre … strange. But then there were writ-
ings that were magnificent. My mother was wonderful, loving, bright,
upbeat, ahead of her time and intelligent. When other women were
going through tough times, she would assemble packets for them and

include her own inspirational messages. She wanted to help them, and she often did. She saved her other essays in pocket folders, hoping they would eventually be read by others who were living a hellish nightmare similar to the one that she was living.

As for Nick and I, after our wonderful honeymoon, reality started to set in: Nick had a fiery personality. But I was *crazy in love* with him. I knew about his bad temper before my *Princess Wedding* because while we were dating, he had hit me a few times, but I thought he would settle down after we married. After he hit me, he said he felt bad and would make up with me and promise not to do it again. But it would happen again.

Unfortunately, Nick's temper was just a part of who he was at that time. He was jealous and would just "blow" if another man looked at me, and he would take his anger out on me. There was one night I'll never forget. He was all stirred up about something, and he kept pushing me down on the bed. I said something to divert him, and I ran out of the small apartment. It was late in the evening, and I ran down the hall and knocked on someone's apartment door. I pleaded to be allowed to come inside, and I telephoned my brother-in-law. My brother-in-law arrived and was ready to go and have a word with Nick, but all I wanted to do was get out of there. *Just leave it.* Nick called me the next day to tell me how sorry he was and, once again, promised it would not happen. After that, we moved into a house together, but it didn't stop. During another episode of his anger, I finally realized that one of these days he could seriously hurt me, and so I left the house with just the clothing I was wearing and went to my parent's house. My mom and dad opened their doors and were happy to have me back in a safe place, but it was a very unhappy ending for me. One more time, Nick tried to get me back, but I was done and filed for divorce. (By the way, people can change, and Nick eventually did.)

In the 70s, Catholics weren't allowed to divorce, and I was banned from the Catholic Church. I couldn't even walk into the church and I thought to myself, "Wait a minute … what about forgiving? This is a time in my life when I need help, and you're telling me I can't come into the church." That made no sense to me. I never went into the Catholic Church again, and I felt lost for years with no religion to hang on to. During this time, I struggled because I was not able to instill a religious foundation in my little children. I felt guilty that I could not give them all the tools they needed for a full life.

Finally, in 1992, when living in Virginia Beach, I accepted Christ as my Savior. I attended a Baptist church after David Meinz, a professional speaker and spiritual mentor in my life, invited me to attend services with him. This took quite a bit of convincing on David's part as these two religions are at opposite ends of the spectrum. In fact, when I was young I always heard from nuns and priests, "If you go into a Baptist church, you will burn in hell!" Do you get the irony of this? Eventually David Meinz became a spiritual leader for *my* Dave, too.

Many years later, when my husband Dave was so sick battling pancreatic cancer and I was taking care of him round-the-clock, I thought of my dad and how, among other things, his once-thriving business declined because of my mother's illness. It is very difficult to run a business when a loved one has a long-term illness or devastating disease. It is extremely difficult to keep your focus on work, which your livelihood depends upon if you're an entrepreneur. Demands are somewhat different if you have a self-sustaining business, but even then, the owner has to be involved if the business is to survive. I felt *the truth of this* pressing on me often when Dave was ill and I was operating Office Dynamics. I had to keep my focus. How could I when my spouse was deathly ill and I had to call his doctors and make his chemotherapy appointments? I was his driver. I hate to say it, but because of my father's formidable experiences, I knew what I had to do. Failure was not an option because it would result in financial ruin. Later, I looked back with pride: not only did I attend to Dave's every need, but I also operated Office Dynamics International successfully, and the business actually grew.

Life has so many disruptions—some minor, others major. The major ones deliver a one-two punch and knock me for a loop. There were times when I felt like I was floating through space observing a movie about someone else. This could not really be happening to me, my husband or a child … could it? But it was, and so I would just coast through the day the best I could, and eventually I would feel "normal." It was a new normal.

My mom and my dad are very important to me in terms of how I gathered my strength. They were my inspiration and role models. When Dave was sick and I couldn't bear it, I would talk to my dad, and he would say you just have to make it through today. "Don't think about tomorrow. Don't think about three months from now. Just make it through today."

My dad had been through a lot. He lost his mother when he was fourteen; two of his three siblings died before they were twenty-one. He was always proud about being successful even though he didn't graduate from high school. He suffered with Paget's disease (a form of bone cancer), had open heart surgery and numerous operations. My dad is a paragon of mental strength. I know I come from good stock!

He's always been a fighter and has a phenomenal attitude. Because of that, as of the writing of this book, my dad is still running his business at eighty-seven years of age!

Chapter Two

Be BOLD...
Put the Spotlight
on the BIG Life-Five
Wellness, Financial, Spiritual, Family & Career

"When I stand before God at the end of my life,
I would hope that I would not have a single bit of talent left, and
could say, I used everything you gave to me."
—ERMA BOMBECK

The BIG Life, examined ...

Some eighty-year-old people Live a BIG Life, and other eighty-year-old people don't. None of us knows how long we're going to live. An individual's winning approach to life and not her longevity enables her to Live a BIG Life. From time to time we read about a teenager who died, and we discover this young person lived a BIG Life.

Quality is important. Whatever you do ... do it well! Each day is important. Each day I ask myself, "How do I support others? How do I inspire others? How do I affect others? How do I uplift others?" When my actions leave me feeling fulfilled instead of empty, I know I'm living a BIG Life. We have a great big beautiful world, and yet, some people don't want to travel. They don't even want to go out of state. And I'm thinking, "Are you kidding? You should see the deserts and the mountains. You should see the oceans." I, too, have to expand my horizons a little more. I've been asked to go to London to speak. I've been asked to go to Africa. There's this speck of fear dancing around inside of people, and many resist taking in the marvels of our big, beautiful planet! It's wonderful when you travel across our country too because it's all different.

The BIG Life for me includes doing what is important to me and doing it well. I believe that God has blessed each of us with some talent. We're not here to just *hang out*. We're here for a reason. Each person has a special gift. Dave was wonderful with details and the operations side of business. Shakespeare told us that the world is a stage and we each have our roles to play. In order to embrace the BIG Life, you must find out what makes you special. What is your unique gift that you must deliver to the world? We each have this *something* in our DNA. Yours is different from mine. Mine is different from my neighbors'. When you find your unique gift and leverage it, the hours of the day go by almost without notice. What you're doing is natural to you, and therefore it's easy. You're in this kind of happy zone, and you're at peace. Writing for you *fills me up* and buoys my BIG Life!

Envision a large and magnificent building supported by five pillars. Remove or weaken one of the pillars, and the building is less sturdy or tumbles to the ground. I have come to realize that a BIG Life is supported by Wellness, Financial, Spiritual, Family and Career pillars. When I tend to each pillar, my BIG Life is intact.

WELLNESS

I was raised in an Italian family, and we loved to eat. I loved to eat. I tried not to think of myself as "overweight," but instead I was voluptuous! However, in my teens and twenties, I became self-conscious over my full figure and tried all kinds of crazy diets: a beef diet, the Atkins diet. One doctor gave me some diuretic-like pills, so I was constantly running to the restroom at work, and I think he may have even prescribed some diet pills. I'd lose all the weight and gain it back. I wore suit jackets even when the temperature was ninety degrees because I wanted to hide my size.

My weight changed when Dave and I moved away from Cleveland. We moved to South Carolina, and I wasn't having those Sunday dinners where we would sit around all day and eat and drink wine. Remember too when you grow up in the Midwest, you have eight months of winter when it's dark, gloomy and cold. You want hot breads and mashed potatoes with gravy and stews: warming food. I changed my habits when we headed south. I stopped eating fried foods. We were able to be outside and physically active most of the time. I started to lose weight and kept it off. I started to feel better and became conscious that if I ate a little too much … too many Oreo cookies, I would gain weight. So I didn't cheat myself out of those foods because eventually a person will over eat those delightful goodies. *Oh, I want a little piece of cake.* I'd have a little piece of cake. If I want to have a cookie at night, I'll have a cookie, not half a bag of Oreos, which I've been known to eat. If Dave were here, he would tell you that he weighed less than I did when we got married. I would not only eat my dinner, but I would finish food on his plate. I was just a happy, little Italian girl. What can I say? After I changed my habits, I felt better, had more energy and more confidence. To this day I'm still very cautious about what I eat. I enjoy a dish of ice cream, but I stay away from fried foods, and here in the southwest, we frequently cook on the grill so that less fat makes it to our plates.

I've paid special attention to nutrition because when I had an emergency abdominal complete hysterectomy in 2006, it zapped my energy. Fortunately I was in better shape than most women at that time, and I can't imagine how much longer my recovery would have taken had I not been in an enviable state of wellness. We choose whether we'll have donuts for breakfast or instead start the day with scrambled egg whites and nice fresh tomatoes. It doesn't have to be difficult; we're choosing wellness.

Attitude plays a role in wellness too. You could be healthy and feel energetic, but if you have a sour attitude, it's going to be your Achilles Heel. If you hold grudges, for example, they gnaw away at you, and you can't be the best version of you. What do you think about all day? Do you hang around with people who talk about depressing things going on in the world? Or do you spend more of your time with people who give you a boost and lift your spirits? I know what's going on in the world, but most of the time I choose not to dwell on the negative. I choose to be a positive force in the world. In order to do this, I need to take care of myself.

I like to support my church when I can. I bring meals to our church where they actively support families who live in shelters or people who are housed at our church for a week a few times during the year because they do not have jobs or homes. One year, I participated in a "Beautify Our Community" project. A group of us went to a place known as Opportunity Village to paint little Christmas-like houses that had become worn. (Opportunity Village is a not-for-profit organization that serves people in our community who have intellectual disabilities in order to enhance their lives and the lives of the families who love them. Opportunity Village is dedicated to helping people with severe intellectual and related disabilities become the very best they can be.) First, we had to scrub wooden walls with hard bristle brushes and buff surfaces, and then we painted them with red, white and green paints. We were working in ninety-degree temperatures. I lasted four hours and finally said to the younger people, "I have to go." I was able to participate as many hours as I did because I purposely keep myself strong and healthy (and also because of God's grace). I love to swim and play with my grandchildren. I like to take long walks viewing the beautiful mountains that surround my neighborhood, hike in Red Rock Canyon with my family or walk on the beach, which is my favorite place of all. If I'm not taking care of myself, I'd be cheating myself out of these opportunities.

Another approach to wellness is to get therapeutic massages. From time to time, women have told me, "I don't want a stranger touching my body." That kind of thinking *feeds the dragon*. It prevents further investigation, which leads to making decisions without sufficient information. What I'm talking about is therapeutic massage. I prefer deep tissue massage. All these toxins build up in our bodies when we have stress. If you're at a desk or a computer all day like I am, sometimes, all you need is one hour with the right masseuse. Afterward, I'm like Jell-O, a bouncy gelatin dessert. All of a sudden my head is clear, and the tension is gone. I'm refreshed, and, with all the toxins released, I can be better at what I'm going to do that day.

Women don't make enough time for themselves. We are really good at taking care of everyone else who is important to us and touches our lives. We want to be there for everybody, and we can't be there for everybody. People live longer today, and so many women are raising their own kids and taking care of aging parents at the same time. I hear many women in their fifties or sixties say that their grown children are going through messy divorces, and they are helping take care of the grandchildren or incurring the financial debt that goes along with hiring lawyers and more. Or they tell me that their adult children have moved back home because they lost their own houses or their jobs.

Today's women are just going to have to learn to take care of themselves. For years I've heard women say, "I can't go sit in a bubble bath for thirty minutes, my kids need me." You know what? You can go and sit in a bubble bath; you'll be a better mother, the kind your kids need you to be. Or women I knew would go to the spa with a friend or have lunch and feel guilty. What good is that? It almost nixes the entire point of why you took that day for yourself. When you do that you're … *feeding the dragon*. Other people pick up on that theme. Since I was a young wife and mother, I believed that if I didn't take care of me, then I couldn't be the best for everyone else. I could not be a great employee, a loving and caring wife, a good and loving mother, daughter, sister, neighbor or friend. I believe taking care of ourselves is the greatest gift we can offer so that we can be there to support those who need us most. We've got to use positive language. *I deserve this time. I'm allowed to take care of myself.*

I'm sharing the following with you to *keep it real* … admittedly I wasn't doing any of the above when Dave was very sick. I kept a pretty grueling pace with Dave, and that's putting it mildly. I was up at 4:00 AM putting in a full day with my work and traveling, but it would be nothing for me to still be awake at 10:00 at night or awake and be with him at 3:00 in the morning, and for seven months we were running back and forth bi-weekly to the hospital and doctors in California. I did pretty well, but after a while it started to take a toll on my body, especially during the last six months of Dave's life. I mustered every bit of energy I could because that's what we do when we're in a crisis situation. The body knows how to *pull-up*. We get into that fighting mode, but after the crisis, we crash. I experienced that crash (called post-traumatic stress) once before, after Office Dynamics hosted our Annual Conference for Administrative Excellence in 1999. We were in Virginia Beach when Hurricane Floyd made an appearance (you can read more about this in Chapter Ten).

During the final eight weeks of Dave's life, I was frequently light-headed and feeling the physical effects of the situation. I was dehydrated, nauseous and could not think straight, but I couldn't stop to take care of myself. And we were hosting our 17th Annual Conference for Administrative Excellence in Las Vegas, which is a three-day event but requires many weeks of preparation. I was exhausted and every day felt anxious asking myself, "Is Dave going to make it? What if he passes away the day before my event? What will happen? Who will present my speeches? How will I handle all the chaos? Or what if he is so sick, I can't leave him?" Our plan was for Dave to rest at home while I was hosting this conference, which is a big event for us. Assistants come from around the world. But Dave had been a part of our conference for the last two years since he was an Office Dynamics employee during that time. The first morning of our event, I woke up and walked toward the bathroom only to find Dave in our walk-in closet half crunched over trying to dress himself. He didn't have an ounce of physical energy to spare. I asked, "What are you doing?"

He said, "I'm going to your conference." He knew this would be the last Office Dynamics conference he would witness, and he was determined and stubborn enough to say to his cancer, "You are not going to stop me!" I was constantly amazed at the strength Dave could bring forth when his mind was made up. I helped him get dressed and then dressed myself. My daughter, Lauren, was already scheduled to attend our event, and so she stayed by her dad's side that entire day helping him get around in a motorized wheelchair. From the big stage up front, I could see this little weak, thin man who was my husband of thirty-four years smiling with pride at what I had accomplished with my company. Dave was always proud of who I had become, even though he was not at all supportive of me and my business at the onset and during the first two years. Later, he became my biggest fan, and I'm sure by now you can tell that we had a strong marriage. It was not always easy mind you … but strong and with a deep level of love. (Note: Today, many couples don't want to work things out. And many men and women don't want to commit to marriage until they test it for several years. Why is that?) You never know what will happen until you jump in with both feet, and that is very scary. But that is how you Live a BIG Life that is filled with the clouds and bright sunshine.

Soon after hosting that conference, my health got so bad I went to my doctor. It was the last day of our conference. I was standing on the stage and had a half-day to go, but I felt so faint. I was pushing through my speeches praying to God to please let me make it four more hours. I could hardly stand as I looked out at 240 attendees. They had no idea what was going on within me or that Dave was coming to the end of his life. When the conference ended, I attended our Office Dynamics staff lunch to celebrate a very successful conference. I was beyond exhaustion that Friday night. Dave and I went to sleep, and when we woke up, he was attempting to get dressed once again. This time he wanted to put on his "army-like" pants and tee-shirt. For six months, almost all Dave wanted to discuss was … camping. He loved to camp when he was a little boy, and we used to camp all the time when our kids were little. Hospice personnel had told me that when a person is close to passing, he or she reflects on childhood memories and things that made him feel good, safe and loved. Something else had transpired during his "I am traveling the country and in camping mode" (even though Dave could not get out of bed). He had talked about purchasing a red Jeep. His mind was set, and there was no talking him out of it. So that Saturday morning, right after my conference, I traipsed off with him to visit a Jeep dealer. We walked around the lot, or should I say, I sat in a corner feeling horrible and angry at Dave about this Jeep ordeal, but I was *hurting* and not mentally up to par. He walked around, found his red Jeep and before I knew what had hit me, I was signing papers for a brand new Jeep. By the way, I hated that particular model. It provided no-frills transportation that was just the thing for a rugged, outdoorsman individual. It certainly was not my vehicle of choice. I was accustomed to my Cadillac … a luxurious CTS Cadillac that I gave up so he could get this Jeep. What was I thinking? Well, I wasn't (thinking) because I was so sick. Dave was happy as a lark. At the time, the plan was that I would drive Dave's other gorgeous high-end SUV (also a Jeep) and he would drive the new shiny, red Jeep. But in the end, it did not work out like I thought. After Dave passed away, I was stuck with two vehicles. Because he had not signed over the really nice SUV to me as a beneficiary, I could not keep that vehicle. Actually he did sign it over two days before he died, but because I was busy with him approaching his end, I did not send in the paper thinking I will send it afterward. I learned later it actually had to be submitted before he died. So I could not keep the vehicle I loved, and I was stuck with a vehicle I hated with payments! Boy was I in a pickle. Finally, on February 25, 2011 (my son's birthday), my fantastic Chief Executive Assistant, Jasmine Freeman, spent the entire day with me at the Jeep dealership offloading the two vehicles, writing a check for $10,000 and culminating with me driving away with a nicely used 2010 Jeep just like Dave's old fancy one but with no extras and a low monthly payment.

Going back to what happened with me due to my lack of health situation, my doctor had to hydrate me for several hours, and I was told to go home and rest. *Yeah right.* While Family Health provided nurses to assist with Dave, they only took care of the basics and came three to four days a week for about forty-five minutes. Also, men seem to be really stubborn about having another woman take care of them. Even though Dave needed help with baths or a shower, he refused to let a nurse help.

He only wanted my help. So I did the best I could. I focused on taking vitamins and still take vitamins. After Dave passed, there was a huge emotional toll on my body. Remember what I said about post-traumatic stress. I was getting pretty good at identifying the symptoms now, letting it flow through my body and mind (instead of fighting it) and knowing it would eventually pass.

Six months later I thought, "Okay, now it's my turn." I finally joined Lifetime Fitness, which I absolutely love. Even though I belong to a country club and there's a gym available to me, I wanted to exercise where a lot of people work out, and I hired a trainer to teach me the appropriate exercises based on my fitness goals and age. I did not want to injure myself. I needed a coach and knew it. I found one who is phenomenal! Cody is a young married guy, and he's *all about muscle*. When I am tired or feel like quitting after twenty repetitions, Cody will say, "Come on, you can do five more." And I'll say, "Are you serious?" I groan, and then I do five more and realize he is right. And then after I do, we give each other a *high five* and I feel proud. It is a great feeling for me to push beyond what I think is my limit. I'm committed to spending this time at the fitness center. I run into people from our neighborhood, and the social aspect of being there is a bonus. Also, because I don't like to eat at home by myself too often, I frequently stay and eat at their fabulous café. I can order a healthy meal and enjoy the beautiful view of the Red Rock Mountains. On the days I push myself to go to Lifetime Fitness after work when I am physically and mentally drained, I'm rewarded with a nice boost of energy. After my workout, I also notice an increase in mental sharpness. I recently read that people who work out early in the morning sleep better than people who work out at the end of the day. But my preference is definitely *after work*. Tensions melt, and life feels good!

I hired another coach to assist me with my career. I believe it's possible to benefit from working with a coach on any of the Five Pillars that support a BIG Life.

Consider Working With A Coach

Your initial thought may be, "I can't afford it." At the same time, maybe you can't afford to miss this opportunity. The "right" financial coach, career or wellness coach should help you to achieve your goals. Presumably you'll work smarter and not harder. It may be that a coach will even assist you to *shoot for the stars* when you were ready to aim lower. I don't always like what I hear from my coaches, even when I know they are right. I have coached and am often requested to coach executive assistants on fine tuning areas of their work processes, interpersonal skills, gaining more confidence, or their image. As that outsider, I quickly see what needs to be addressed and what behaviors need fine tuning. Sometimes I have to deliver hard messages, even having to tell women their attire is not the most professional for their level of executive support. It's hard for me to deliver the message. So as women, we need coaches in our lives, and we have to know when to coach others even when it hurts. When a potential coach has practical experience and not simply theoretical know-how to impart, you may just have found a good coach. There are other attributes to look for too. If you want to work with a business coach, is the person you want to work with active in your industry? Is he or she an author or a recognized expert? Does this individual belong to a professional organization (e.g., WABC ... Worldwide Association of Business Coaches)? Members of associations typically have some formal training and pledge to adhere to general standards of professionalism. Does a colleague you admire work with a coach? That individual may be able to answer some questions about working with coaches and may be able to make a recommendation.

I also found a physician I really like who is aligned with MDVIP, a concierge-type service. His focus is on preventative care. It costs more out-of-pocket for this kind of care, but I believe I'm worth it. When women tell me they don't have health insurance, *I don't get it.* Stretch your pocket a little! Give up that daily $5 Latte and resist those magazines at the grocery store check-out counter. Do what it takes to buy coverage and care. If you don't have your health, you can't do the things you love to do. Health has got to be in the forefront. This does not mean we will never face a disease, cancer or illness, but it certainly can help prevent it. Why take a chance? And if something were to happen such as needing an operation, you will recuperate much faster. In one of the MDVIP newsletters, I read worrisome figures: Anxiety Disorders are the most common mental illness in the United States. More than forty million adults fall into this category. More Americans suffer from depression than coronary heart disease, cancer and AIDS combined. Many people who suffer don't realize it. Women tend to say, "Oh it's nothing," when questioned about some physical complaints they suffer long-term (e.g., headaches, inability to sleep). Think of these symptoms as a caution or yellow light. Don't be quick to accept the explanation … *it's nothing.* No one can Live a BIG Life if she is depressed or otherwise in poor health. Information about health and wellness is everywhere. Read. Stay informed. Ask questions. Your physician should be able to answer them for you. I obtain information from varied sources. One valuable source is the Centers for Disease Control (CDC) in Atlanta, GA. I'm referencing several sources near the end of this book.

I'm a firm believer in being pro-active. I read something positive each day, and I've done this for years. I don't wait until I'm *down in the dumps* to pull out an inspirational book. I *feed my mind* daily. And speaking of being pro-active, when we were living in Michigan and I was about forty years old, I was advised by a doctor to have a hysterectomy. I kept telling the doctor, "No way." I realized I would go through instant menopause, and I thought at my age that could be a big mistake. I went in search of information and found a wonderful book, "No More Hysterectomies" by Dr. Christiane Northrup. She had written that too many of these surgeries are needlessly performed. After I read the book from cover-to-cover, I had a list of fourteen questions to ask the doctor, and we agreed to hold off on the surgery as long as possible since I would be heading into my peripause years. (It's such fun being a woman, right?) Fifteen years later, I did have a hysterectomy. My gynecologist found a huge mass when she examined me during a routine checkup. She called for an ultrasound follow-up, and that very night she called me at my home to say, "We must get this out now!" We did. But I was hosting a big conference in two weeks, and it had to wait until after the conference. I wasn't trying to avoid the inevitable, but I was making choices. Even though your doctor urges you to act in a particular way, it's your life, and if it's to be a BIG Life, you have to remember it's your body and you should do your research. No matter how accomplished and well-meaning your doctor is, he or she is only human.

Having the right people in our lives is important to our wellness. As a friend of mine said, "Your inner circle is there to support you, Joan, when you feel like you can't take one more dose of bad news or heartache." Who is your inner circle? Do you have friends, family or even close business professionals you can reach out to? Life would be very difficult for me without my inner circle.

FINANCIAL

There are statistics that tell us women outlive men by five to seven years, and yet so many women are naïve about money and family finances. For years, the way Dave and I lived our lives was fabulous. We were both very successful in our careers. We took exciting vacations together. Dave's dad died young, so when Dave and I first married we listened to people say, "When I retire, this … when I retire, that," but we weren't going to wait around until we retired. Dave's dad saved and saved and finally purchased a little dream house on an island for him and Dave's mom. Soon afterward Dave's dad was diagnosed with Alzheimer's disease. We weren't going to squander our monies, but we were going to live life! You already know that Dave was diagnosed with pancreatic cancer at age fifty-six, and he died at age sixty.

Women should be involved ... know what's going on with m-o-n-e-y! All adults (especially heads of households) should know about every aspect of personal finances. Dave would tell me, "You need to get your nose in here and see what I'm doing." Dave owned two LLCs (i.e., Limited Liability Corporations) and two investment properties, and he was overseeing other income-producing ventures (e.g. stocks, bonds, investment portfolio). Dave owned one of the investment properties with my dad. The deed on the other house was in Dave's name only. While that loan was in his name only, I had to file a joint return for the year in which he passed and was responsible for paying taxes on it. Did I know the passwords associated with Dave's various accounts? I did not! Were monies set aside to pay quarterly taxes? Were anticipated contributions to retirement accounts planned, and if so, where were those monies parked? Dozens and dozens of questions arose, and Dave was in no condition to answer them. So not only was I *over-the-top* with worry about Dave's battle with cancer, but I was under immeasurable stress for six months until we established a clear picture of Dave's financial holdings and responsibilities. In some cases, only Dave's name was on sensitive documents, and my attorney had to get involved with settlement of affairs on my behalf.

One bright spot in all of this is Stephanie Roxbury. Stephanie is *an angel from heaven*. She's a fine bookkeeper, and Dave wanted to hire her after reading her advertisement in a local newspaper. Dave was a *numbers guy*, and he interviewed Stephanie. I dragged my heels about meeting with Stephanie, but thankfully she worked with Dave for a short time before he became too sick to explain things to me or to anyone. Stephanie knew some of Dave's passwords for accessing information on the computer. She worked on some of our personal tax returns and she knew about the tenants in the two houses and about money coming in and money going out. There were four or five bank accounts that Stephanie knew about. She was my salvation! Stephanie continues to work with me. (Stephanie's name appears with four others in this book under the heading: *my angels from heaven.* I have nothing but admiration for all of them: Jasmine Freeman, Michele Busch, Nancy Fraze and my sister, Gina DeGirolamo, who has been by my side since Dave was diagnosed with pancreatic cancer.)

One of my favorite sayings is, "Who you are today is not yet all of who you are capable of becoming." If you don't currently oversee family finances, and you think, "Oh this can wait," be advised, it cannot wait. If you're thinking, "Well, we're young, this can wait." Be advised, it cannot wait. Accidents, illness and death can strike at any age. In order to Live a BIG Life, be smart about finances!

My dad and I had to sell the house that he owned with Dave. The real estate market was depressed, and the *house was upside down $100,000.* This added an entirely new dimension of stress to my life and put me in a real predicament. This was the first time in my life that my father and I were at odds with each other, and I was worried that it would ruin my relationship with my dad and stepmom forever after. That didn't happen! Nine months after Dave died, we sold that house. The other house sold, too.

The immediate money concerns passed, but then I had to plan for my future as a party of one. I needed help. I talked to someone at the local Charles Schwab Investments office. I asked lots of questions. I interviewed numerous people at the bank and other investment houses, and I obtained references. I couldn't put my trust in just anyone who had a sign announcing his or her financial expertise and was well dressed, well groomed and well spoken. It's too easy to *believe* someone is competent just because he or she says so. I called my brother-in-law, Bob, who always had a good head on his shoulders when it comes to money matters. At a very deep level, it dawned on me that I could get all this insight from others, but the bottom line is nobody is responsible for me but me. I had to make the decisions that would either reap rewards, or I would pay the price big time.

And there's more: every woman should have a good attorney "on call." I kept pushing Dave to set up a trust, and he procrastinated. Suddenly he got so sick we thought he was dying. Dave knew he had to set his affairs in order and sign some property over to me. I had to go get Power of Attorney papers from my new lawyer, find a notary and get Dave's signature. This was the last thing I wanted to do when my husband was so sick. And it was no easy task for either of us. I learned a lot of this the hard way. If your husband has issues with all this legalese, just insist he do it. You've got to take care of business. A woman who lives a BIG Life can do nothing less.

You need a will, too. My mom died a long time ago, and she didn't leave a will or any information about her desires, and she was divorced from my dad. It was up to us daughters to determine whether they should put in a feeding tube, and no one wants to be in that position. It's horrible. Fortunately Dave had a living will, and I knew exactly what his wishes were. The first two times complications arose we took him to the hospital to give him a chance for some longevity, but at the very end it was the last week, and he was getting ready to pass, so it was another matter. It was New Year's Eve Day, and I was in the other room sitting with my kids, and Dave supposedly was in bed and couldn't move easily, so I thought he was secure. He had a walker near his bed and apparently tried to get up and use it, and all of a sudden all I heard was Dave yelling for me. I ran and the kids ran with me. He had fallen against the edge of the dresser and cut his head. We hurried the grandchildren out of the bedroom and called 911. The medics came and wanted to take him to the hospital and I said, "NO." I had to show them Dave's signed, dated and notarized living will. "I know he does not want to linger anymore." This document gave me the confidence to decline for him. The medics checked him to make sure nothing was broken. They tended to the laceration and bandaged it. They left. Dave passed at 11:00 PM on January 3rd. It took more than one hour for the public officials who had to confirm Dave's death to arrive at our home. That's why the death certificate indicates January 4th as the time of death. Our family knows it was January 3rd.

I would be remiss if I didn't mention one more thing at this point. It has nothing to do with finances but rather with the people you love and care for. If you are ever in a hospital for anything, you have to have an advocate. This is somebody who goes to the hospital, visits with you and pays attention to you and the care you receive or don't receive. The advocate speaks on your behalf. There are too many things that can go wrong in a hospital, and when you're the patient, you can't easily get up, get around or chase after the nurses. If you know of anyone who does not have an advocate, go to the hospital and be an advocate for that person. This may sound extreme, and I realize you would need legal standing, but it's so important for anyone in a hospital to have an advocate that I'll risk sounding extreme. If possible, locate someone close to the patient and notify them that an advocate is needed.

I'm not much of a "numbers person," but my goal is to leave a legacy. It's in the early stages of planning, but there will be an entity to continue after I am gone. It shall mesh with my philosophies and values. When I listen to audio messages, I hear financially successful people report there are four stages related to money: preparing to earn it, earning it, providing for your family and yourself, and helping others. I'm at the stage where I want to make more money so that I can give it to others. Office Dynamics donates dollars and personal items to Whitney Elementary

School, which has a student population made up of 85 percent homeless youngsters. We also donate colored markers and pencils for the students to use. The business contributes 10 percent of the proceeds from sales of an earlier book, "UNDERNEATH IT ALL (Postgraduate Level Revelations Lift Administrative Assistants to New Heights)." These monies are sent to the Pancreatic Cancer Action Network. 50 percent of book sales proceeds from, "WHO TOOK MY PEN … AGAIN?" are sent to St. Jude's Children's Hospital. Of course, I personally donate monies to my church and make it known that I am available to talk with people who have loved ones facing the fight against pancreatic cancer. The ultimate of living my BIG Life is the realization that I'm physically able and therefore must help people who don't have the know-how or ability to take care of themselves, who may be missing an arm or a leg, or otherwise laboring under a major hardship. I'm here by God's Grace, and he guides me to give back.

SPIRITUAL

I can say without hesitation that my relationship with God is the most important pillar in my life. My spirituality permeates everything I do and everything I am. When Dave was so very sick, and I was crying and feeling so alone, I knew I wasn't really alone. It was too late to call my sister or my dad, but I could talk to God any time I wanted to. I knew the only way to overcome my fears were to *stare them in the face*. By that I mean to face them head on. I won't permit myself to look the other way or ignore a problem. The sooner I acknowledge the obstacle, the quicker I can act. I may opt to wait or do nothing. But that is a choice made based upon my deliberation. Failure to stare my fears in the face is not an option for me. I may feel shock and grief at first; then I get my bearings and move into fight mode. I become determined that this obstacle will not overcome me because my God is bigger and more powerful than anything that life throws at me. I know I come from good stock. The DeGirolamo family and the Adorney family are families of courage, strength, will and determination.

Chapter Ten in this book is entitled, "My Spirituality & God's Grace." You'll find that I write about my spirituality in many places in this book, and that's true of other *pillars* as well. We're talking about a BIG Life, and it doesn't come in neat little packages. I think you'll agree the following comments relate well to this oh-so-important pillar:

There is a difference between being religious and being spiritual. I often hear people say, "I'm religious. I go to church and I pray." Yet they don't appear to consider turning their problems over to God. They carry their burdens alone. I have done that. I have tried to use my skills and judgment to "make it better or make it go away." As you can see, I'm writing in the past tense. I don't do that anymore. I discovered I like turning my problems over to the most powerful Being.

When I get caught up in monster-sized challenges, I sit quietly and speak to God. I step out of "Joan, the person walking on the Earth" and become "Joan, a living spirit, child of God, who is only on this Earth for a short time." My huge problems shrink. In time, people who have relevant talents appear to support me. And almost as if from nowhere answers come to me; the *weeds in my path* are cleared away and I soon realize I came through it with God's Grace. This is not about me. It's about the most powerful Being who created me and blesses me even when I do not see a way out. I felt the closest to the spirit world the last seven days of Dave's life. I called on Hospice (an organization that trains people how to treat those who are near death in ways that are compassionate for the individual and his or her loved ones). The Hospice counselor told me that dying takes effort. It's hard work. She brought a wonderful book to share with me and our children. Lauren, Wade (my stepson) and I sat at the little kitchen table with her, and I asked what happens to the body. "What will Dave look like? What happens at the last moment when we take our last breath?" Dave was destined to take his last breath in our home, in our bedroom. I wanted to be prepared so that I didn't *freak-out*. I had never seen someone at the exact moment of death. The counselor reviewed the process, and I realized I had already seen seven of the ten predictable changes in Dave. He had been preparing to die for weeks but would not leave because he was determined to have his last Christmas Eve with me and our children and grandchildren.

The counselor told us we had a small window of opportunity to tell Dave anything we wanted to say. Hearing is the last sense to go. So even if he did not respond, we should talk to him. Rarely do people get to have this very intimate time with a loved one (family member or friend) before the individual leaves this world.

This was when I was in that warm place of the spiritual realm. I was not afraid anymore. I was ready to help Dave leave this world and go to his heavenly Father. Our kids were also saying good-bye and telling Dave they would be fine and that he could leave; his hard work was done. He was our warrior and hero and will be forever. Our best friends, John and Ruth, also got to say farewell to Dave. And our neighbor and good friend, Sharyn, was able to talk to him privately. She had been a caregiver for her husband for fourteen years and was now a widow. God was so good to us. What a blessing to have these last days and hours to speak to Dave.

My spiritual journey continues to blossom. I love attending services at The Crossing, a Christian church where I'm a congregant. Eleven years ago, services were held in a high school gym. These days we meet in a huge new facility, which we've essentially outgrown. Preparations are underway to build a new and larger church building. Obviously many people flock to The Crossing, but I don't feel the need to attend weekly services in order to be connected to God. You already know I chat with God from my car, the supermarket, while walking my dogs or working out at the gym.

I am not spared heartaches because I follow the Lord, but I know this connection makes it easier for me to be happy and to live my BIG Life. I can be strong for others who face tough times. I feel good when I help others. The fact is my own challenges seem less overwhelming when I provide words of encouragement to others. Helping others is a rewarding "job."

FAMILY

From the time I was a little girl, family has been important to me. In the Italian culture, family is very strong. I was raised with Italian cousins and grandparents, and the family always came first. My dad told us that "blood is thicker than water," and when times are tough friends may desert you, but your family will be there for you. I loved spending time with my family when I was young, and today it is still one of my favorite pastimes. We can just be gathered in the living room talking with one another, and I feel happy. I realize that some people don't feel that way about their families, but I'm definitely not in their camp! I get strength from my family and don't think my sisters and I ever had a major blow-up even though we're each very different.

Janet, Gina and I are "blood sisters," and Kelly is our adopted sister. Later in life my parents divorced, and my dad married Liz. Liz is Kelly's mom, and my dad adopted Kelly after he and Liz married. Kelly was thirteen years old, and I'm nineteen years older than Kelly. She is a loving person and was delighted to have sisters. We feel close to one another, but Janet and Gina and I went through so much heartache with our mother that our bond is especially close. Kelly has children of her own now, and I was touched when she participated in a raise-money-for-pancreatic-cancer-research-run in Cleveland, Ohio.

My mother's illness impacted the family. How could it not? It's an illness that scares people because they don't know how to deal with it. Some of my aunts and other family members were there to help my dad.

But no one really knew what to do. Now my dad is a *ball of fire*, and he needed someone in his life like Liz. She is an amazing homemaker who does everything with creativity and care. At holiday time she makes special chocolates and tucks them inside of whimsical coverings that make us smile. We know she loves to do this and so many other things for all of us, and she has been wonderful for my dad. Even though my parents were divorced, Liz would go to my mom's apartment and tidy up for her. No doubt it was Liz's generous nature that gave rise to this unusual dynamic. On holidays my mother and Liz and my dad were all together with the rest of us. I believe that to Live a BIG Life you have to have support from family, from people who love you. And support and love is a reciprocal happening, a two-way street. *You give you receive. You receive you give.*

As I mentioned, my mom attempted suicide three times. I would cry, my dad would shout, and Dave and I finally decided we had to move our children, who were two and three years old, away from this madness. They were being exposed to so much ugliness, and it wasn't healthy for anyone but certainly not for such young children. We were afraid to tell my dad since we knew he would feel hurt. We thought he might yell or cry. I smile when I think of it now, but we were so worried that when we invited Liz and my dad to our home to tell them about our plans, Dave and I sat on the far side of the room! My dad is so sensitive. He said, "If I were you, I would do the same thing." He got it. He understood. I'm very close to my dad and love him very much, and it was a dreadful irony that we moved out of town on his birthday.

Dave's family didn't talk to one another often, and yet they were close. When Dave was so sick and I called my sister-in-law, Barb, who lived out of state, and told her, "You've got to come," she asked if she could come next week. I said, "You've got to come now. I'm scared!" And, in the blink of an eye, she was on a plane coming to us. She stayed at our home for about two weeks, and it was great support for me. She witnessed firsthand what I was going through and would be there at night to eat with us in the bedroom and sip a glass of red wine with me. Dave's mom ended up living with her children. My sister-in-law, Jan, was her caretaker until she could no longer do it. Clearly, the Burge family did the *right thing* for one another.

Dave and I have two dear friends who were (and are) like family to us. When Dave was so sick, Ruth and John were present during our darkest hours. They were at the UCLA Hospital in Los Angeles the day the surgeon told me Dave had pancreatic cancer. And they were by Dave's side at our home until the very end when John walked out the front door to help the coroner put the stretcher holding Dave's body into the van. John, our son Brian, my brother-in-law Pete, Wade, and my son-in-law Jeff all accompanied the coroner when Dave left our beautiful home for the last time.

Ruth lost all of her family when she was young, and she and John don't have grandchildren. They were invited to our house on several Christmas Eves, and they attended the children's birthday parties. Ruth would buy gifts for my granddaughter—the cutest skirts and hats and accessories that little girls treasure. Ruth and John are part of our family and shall be forever. If you're focused on living a BIG Life and don't have *blood relatives* ... you have no need to be concerned. Special friends can love you, listen to you, laugh with you, help to get you through the tough times and help you to celebrate the best of times just like a sister, brother, aunt or uncle would or could do.

One of my cousins never married. She's a very successful businesswoman and very attractive, and when she was fifty years old she decided to adopt a child. She adopted a little girl from Vietnam. A few years later she adopted another little girl. She and the girls are a loving family. My cousin lives a BIG Life.

Pets belong in my FAMILY PILLAR! When Lauren and Brian were each less than ten years old, Dave announced that he wanted to own a big dog. I didn't *warm to the idea* since working full time and raising two children was enough for me. Earlier in our marriage we had cocker spaniels. Our first was a gorgeous black dog, and we called her Lady. She was easy to love because she was a lady! She joined our family when we lived in Cleveland. When we moved to North Carolina and had a beautiful home with a beautiful yard, Lady got into a habit that proved to be a problem. Our yard property backed up to a farm, and the farmer owned cows. We didn't know this until after we were in the house. Lady would trek over there and roll in some nasty stuff. When she came home she smelled awful and needed to be thoroughly hosed off and hosed off quickly. It got to be a lot of work, and so my wonderful in-laws agreed to let Lady come live with them. When we moved to Memphis, we took ownership of another cocker spaniel. This canine bore no resemblance to Lady! She knocked over and broke things. One time, she jumped on my kitchen counter and helped herself to a barbecued chicken leg. She ran around my immaculate new home dropping red sauce on the light-colored carpet. You can see why I was "over it" when Dave mentioned getting a big dog to live with us. I knew that Dave envisioned a pet sitting next to his chair at night or walking with him in the woods across the street. I thought to myself, "Who am I to tell him no?" So naturally I told him, "Okay." One day he came home with the cutest, chubbiest little golden retriever, and I *took to* her immediately. I fell in love with Annie, who grew to be a rather large golden retriever who would happily eat anything in sight including toilet paper and a frozen steak she got from the top of the kitchen counter. She was the love of our household and my big cuddle dog. After several years, we decided Annie needed a companion. Dave and I were away from home during the work week and so Zoe, another golden retriever, joined our family. Annie and Zoe moved to Las Vegas with us, but eight months after we moved we had to *put both of them down* due to cancer. I missed Annie terribly since I felt so connected to her. When I was home for weeks recuperating from my hysterectomy, she laid on the side of my bed. Whenever Dave or I didn't feel well, she was right there to comfort us. A few months after she passed, we got another golden retriever we named Tessa. And after Zoe passed, we got another golden retriever and named her Charday. Charday is like a mini-version of Annie and is playful and fun-loving. Tessa's personality is much like that of Zoe. They are great company to me now that I live alone in the house. My golden retrievers help me to live my BIG Life. They don't answer back, they love me unconditionally, listen to all my gibberish, make me laugh and welcome me home after a long day. They keep me company. By all means, they belong in this FAMILY PILLAR.

How could we ever have canines in our home without having a trusted someone to call upon when they needed attention and we weren't home? Meet Don. Don came into our lives soon after we moved to Las Vegas. We were introduced to him by our friends John and Ruth. They hired Don to clean homes they had for sale and serve as a handyman too. He even cleaned their home. They warned us that Don had a knack for breaking things ... nice things. He would hide the damage by gluing parts of vases back together or otherwise making repairs. He would not get around to mentioning the *incidents* until many months after they occurred. We hired Don to clean our home and be our handyman. He installed all the fan lights in our new house, and to this day is at my house in a heartbeat to assist with any maintenance issue or to touch-up paint on a house that is now showing the signs of age. Don is the full-time sitter for my two golden retrievers. His friend Janice loves Tessa and Charday too. They are amazing people with their love and care for *my girls*. They watch out for me too, and I trust them 100 percent with my pets and my home. They would cook meals when Dave was sick. Don was there when Dave had to *put down* our beloved Annie. I say without hesitation I could not Live a BIG Life without Don and Janice.

Yes, Don has broken a few items, and it took him months to tell me the vacuum sucked up the lovely delicate drapery in my bathroom. I finally noticed that one side of the beautiful draping looked ragged, and I was curious about what must have happened. Remember … I travel often and don't always pay careful attention to every little item in the house. Don thought he would use the vacuum to clean the very delicate designer fabric … and, as they say, the rest is history. Sometimes we have to overlook the little things people do that might annoy or upset us and look at the big picture: all the good they bring into our lives. To Live a BIG Life we have to forgive and to focus on the strengths and gifts people bring to us because of who they are. We have to overlook the little stuff and focus on how life would be shallower or "less than" without that person. I would not be who I am today without hundreds of people coming into my life during my adult years on Earth. I know I'm not naming all of them, but if you're reading this book and are looking for your name, please don't be disappointed. I know who you are and you do too. Thank You!

CAREER

My uncle owned three hundred beauty salons all doing business in various states. When I was twelve and thirteen, I worked in his salons in Cleveland, Ohio. I would sweep the floors, collect the money from the guests and make change. When I went to high school, I moved on to work at Franklin Ice Cream. It was wonderful because I loved to eat at that time and I could eat all the ice cream I wanted. I made large sundaes for myself, and my employer encouraged me. "Enjoy! Enjoy!" I also worked part-time at a ladies dress shop. I always wanted to work and have some money of my own.

When I was in my early twenties, I was fortunate to work for TRW Inc., a fantastic large corporation. I was also extremely lucky to have one executive during the second part of my career with TRW who was a mentor and coach to me. He was my "boss" as we said in those days. His name is John Guinness, and he had a tremendous influence on me. To this day, I don't think John knows how much I learned from working with him and watching him operate as a highly successful executive. He was smart, handsome and sharp, and admired by men and women alike. He had a reputation for being a rebel, and that appealed to the twenty-something Joan! John made it clear to everyone that I deserved respect as an administrative assistant. Our one-on-one morning meetings were not to be disturbed. In his charming British accent, he let everyone know I was important to the smooth operation of his affairs. Imagine how I felt at such a young age. There are many executive assistants today who don't want to "bother" the executives they support because executives are too busy. Not so with John Guinness. He created a kind of team-cocoon that made me feel secure and important and enabled me to do my job well.

In the large corporate setting, I learned to work with dozens of personality-types. I supported fascinating executives and was introduced to beautiful places where I frequently met other VIP executives. I had lots of fun at company events, parties and picnics. I traveled on a corporate jet one time, which was the highlight of my career as an assistant. All this time I was focused on my career … I never spoke of it as a "job" … it was not a job … it was my career.

In 1990, there was not one company that specialized in training administrative professionals. Companies such as CareerTrack, Skillpath and the American Management Association did not carve out a niche that focused on training administrative professionals, and so there it was right in front of my nose and ripe for picking. That's the good news. The not-such-good-news is company management rarely invested in learning opportunities for this segment of employees. Going forward was tough, but I was tougher! I had tons of faith and knew "someday" my hard work would pay off. I had an inner burning desire (I think God was pushing me) to do this work.

When you act like you know what you're doing, even when you don't, you project a powerful aura. When I first started to speak professionally I was petrified and thought I was going to faint. I was going to speak in front of two hundred people, and I only had a half-hour speech. I thought, "Okay so I'm going to faint on stage, and they won't hire me again." But I knew I would not die!

People tend to look at a barrier and think about giving up. They give up their dreams! I meet a barrier with a question: How badly do I want this? If you want it enough to dig deep and push hard, then ask another question. How can I get around the barrier? It's impossible to lead a BIG Life if you run away from everything all the time. When I'm in a tough spot, I draw on my problem solving skills. I embrace my creativity and examine the situation from different aspects. I'll call people who don't know me, but I'll call them through the National Speakers Association or through some group that has members who may have experience dealing with similar challenges. People in the National Speakers Association don't necessarily know each other, but they're always ready to help. "Okay Joan, what do you need?" It may come to pass that you can't satisfy needs immediately. You need time to prepare to get around that barrier. Do you need some more training? It may be that you need to partner with a more experienced person in order to win an assignment. There's more than one approach to moving ahead, and the woman who insists on living a BIG Life will find one that works! I found Linda Miles when Office Dynamics Ltd. was new. Linda coached me on how to start and operate a business. She gave me an introduction to the business of speaking, but she didn't listen to me speak. I learned from Linda how to produce my first audio tape and how to grow my company.

I met one woman who set up a barrier for herself, and she didn't recognize it. The barrier is labeled complacency, or as she put it, "I want to coast." It probably never occurred to her that she had it within her power to Live a BIG Life. She was a seasoned administrative assistant with a well-paid position, and I wanted to shake her! I was engaged to conduct team training at her company, and a small group of employees were discussing how the assistant could better support the executive and how that executive could better work with the assistant. This administrative assistant was about fifty years old, and when it came time for her to contribute something to our exchange she said, "I'm really content, and I want to coast for a while." I asked how long she planned to coast and she answered, "About eight years."

Do you think you're going to remain on a plateau for eight years? Are you living in a glass bubble? Who is to say you're not going to lose your job? What if something dramatic happens to a family member? How do you sit there and assume this? Is your life that vanilla … is it completely without color?

She thought she was doing a good job and that was sufficient. I was called in because company executives knew they had employees who weren't taking the initiative to do anything. This woman was a perfect example. She sat at her desk and crocheted when she didn't have *something to do*. She was a dismissal waiting to happen!

You have Okayed this all along, Mr. Executive. You should have said something from the beginning.

PROFILE IN A NUTSHELL

The modern woman has life coming at her at Mach speed. Parents are living into their 80s and 90s, and frequently daughters are their caregivers. Young adult children are moving back home. Second marriages often result in later-in-life pregnancies. Women who are nearing the end of child-bearing years adopt children and raise them as single parents. It's not unusual for more mature women to have toddlers running around at home. More than 50 percent of today's working women are small business owners. These women are *driven*. Electronic tools tie people to customers and clients more than ever before. This expands an entrepreneur's reach but makes it essential to keep learning and adjusting to new demands. These are awesome challenges. Nowhere in the annals of history have women been called upon to measure up like this! *If you rest, you rust.* Be BOLD: Put the spotlight on the BIG Life-Five (Wellness, Financial, Spiritual, Family & Career) and see what happens. You've got everything to gain and absolutely nothing to lose.

Chapter Three

All About RLP ...
Red Lipstick Power

"Action will lead you forward to the success you deserve."
—GEORGE CLASON, AUTHOR OF "THE RICHEST MAN IN BABYLON"

One day Jasmine shared this observation with me: If you love red lipstick, you're a clear thinker. Red is elemental—the color that literally makes your heart beat faster. So while wearing a red blouse means you want to stand out, wearing a red lip color means you're willing to stand by your every word. Unfortunately we don't have the author's name. You can, however, find many positive references to the color red. Here are just a few found in one resource: in China, red is associated with good luck and fortune. To the Hindu, red symbolizes joy, life, energy and creativity. Red is the highest arc of the rainbow. Red Letter Day refers to a memorable and joyful day. Red plants in the garden attract the eye and are a good choice for areas you want to draw attention to. Red is considered a warm color in landscape design. Its appearance in the garden has an energetic effect. (Source: www.sensationalcolor.com) I glance at these assertions from time to time and better understand my own affection for RED.

///////

I wear red lipstick 98 percent of the time. Many of the women who attend my conferences and presentations notice and ask about it. (I even wear red lipstick when I'm at home on a Saturday cleaning house. Dave would tease me about it.) I wear it unfailingly because it is a power color. It helps me send the message that I'm a confident woman who is equal to any task (well, almost)! It especially speaks to me on the days I awake and don't feel so powerful. As I look in the mirror and put on my red lipstick, I say to myself, "Red Lipstick ON!" This is my internal mantra that helps me draw from within whenever I need to face the current challenge. Admittedly, RL doesn't affect my two golden retrievers. They typically behave as though they hold all the aces!

Nancy Fraze helped to write and edit Level One of my Star Achievement Series® curriculum. I was so busy with Dave I would e-mail her at night, and she would write in big letters "RED LIPSTICK." I would respond, "Okay Nancy, I got it." When I saw those words, I realized, "I can do this!" Red Lipstick ON were code words, a short way of saying, "Pull back from the abyss and focus." I could say, "Red Lipstick ON!" to myself, but it was especially meaningful when it came from *outside*. Left to my own devices, I might not recognize it's time for RED LIPSTICK. In order to Live a BIG Life you can't live in your own little house, your own world. You need people to support you. You need to be alert to what is going on in the big world. Red Lipstick ON! became a clarion call, and to this very day, when I find myself hesitating as I face something formidable, I'll announce it aloud. My office staff and some close friends and family members know exactly what I mean, and when any of them say these words to me they get my undivided attention.

I certainly recognized that I needed RLP when Dave and I were at UCLA. Dave was there to have a Whipple procedure. During a Whipple the top of the pancreas, a portion of the small intestine and part of the bile duct is removed. Sometimes part of the stomach is also removed. I was scared. We didn't yet know whether he had pancreatic cancer, and there we were in this very big hospital to discuss the procedure with Dr. Howard Reber, a highly respected surgeon who performed about one hundred Whipple procedures a year. We were expecting a nine-hour surgery and believed everything was going to be fine. After three hours, Dr. Reber came walking down the long hospital corridor, and I knew something was wrong. He sat down and told me that it was pancreatic cancer and it had spread to a major vein and he couldn't do anything for Dave. I was in total shock. I was panicking but asked, "What next?" He told me Dave had to have chemotherapy and maybe it would shrink the tumor. After that, Dave would return for surgery. He immediately told me we should go to Dr. William Isacoff's office right there at UCLA. You don't just walk into Dr. Isacoff's office; you have to be referred. He devotes his life to pancreatic cancer research and treatment, but he is quirky. He's *out of the box*, and he's also the reason Dave lived as long as he did. The doctor's assistant was wonderful. She prepared me for what to expect. "The doctor isn't very friendly when he speaks to a patient's wife. He might not even look at you."

So imagine how I felt. I thought my husband was dying, and I was in what I call my *Black Hole*. I didn't know anything about this world. I was hearing words like periampullar and duodenojejunostomy. What to do? Who to go to? So when we went for our first appointment, I was petrified and crying and I was a mess. Dr. Isacoff was sympathetic. "We're going to do this for your husband. We're going to get that tumor." We went every two weeks for seven months, and when we went we stayed for two days. I started to realize *as I came back to Earth* that the doctor was often pretty cocky. One day Dr. Isacoff said something about the tumor shrinking. Dave and I asked what the next phase would be, and the doctor got angry. "This is not a phase, and we don't talk about serious stuff as a phase. Quit taking those notes." He took my notebook and hurled it across the room. He said, "You are a smart woman." He and I *got into it*. I shouted, "I am a smart woman and that's why I'm taking notes. I know about my business and certain things, but I know nothing about pancreatic cancer." I believe I gained his respect. He paid attention to me. He talked to me. And I made sure that my RED LIPSTICK was freshly applied whenever we went to see him. I thought, "I don't care who you are. I don't care that you talk to me the way you talk to me or that you're abrupt and short tempered and to the point. I need you and your expertise." That was all that mattered.

I think women in general need to learn to stand their ground. You have to step up to the plate. You can't be afraid to yell back at a doctor, "You're no better than I am. You're a specialist in pancreatic cancer. I know my work. Teach me. I do have questions." You may find yourself dealing with a bully at your office or when communicating with your dry cleaner or advocating for your husband or child. Whenever an occasion calls for some true grit, stand tall! You can't Live a BIG Life without mustering and using strength and tenacity. RED LIPSTICK is a *code phrase*, and I have one other. It popped into my head when I was sitting on the sofa crying my eyes out and Dave was trapped in bed, losing his battle with cancer. "Put on your big girl panties," I chided myself. The next thing I knew I was washing my face and getting ready to take charge of whatever needed that response. (BTW, I recently learned that "Put Your Big Girl Panties on and Deal With It ..." is the name of a book by Roz Van Meter. It's reported to be helpful and humorous.)

Dave was so very sick the last six months of his life, and everything was spinning out of control. Day after day, month after month, the disease was in charge. The only thing I could do was submit to the Lord. I recognized He had a plan. He had a plan for Dave. *You have a far greater plan. I don't have answers. I don't know where; I don't know why. I just submit.* There were days when I wanted to go to an island. I didn't want to face everything. But I had bills to pay, a business to run and a husband who needed me. To submit was humbling, but it was my only option. I knew Dave wasn't going to get better. *How do you stay sane?* My faith in God brought me through this long five-year journey. It began with my emergency hysterectomy, and before that my office was robbed, and then Dave was diagnosed. The doctor's assistant would say to me whatever you have to do together you have to do within the next five years. (The five-year survival rate is only 4 percent.) *Don't tell me my husband is dying within five years. I don't want to hear that. We are young; we are supposed to be together until we are old!*

Patrick Overton wrote, "When you have come to the edge of all light that you know and are about to drop off into the darkness of the unknown, faith is knowing one of two things will happen. There will be something solid to stand on or you will be taught how to fly." I had faith.

Scott Whaley, my Pastor, said the greatest thing to me: "View this as temporary, Joan. This is just a season of your life. This is not the season you'll live in forever. It may be a long season and one you did not choose, but it is temporary." But I would also realize that while I wanted this season to end soon, that also meant that Dave would not be here. Watching someone shrivel away in front of your eyes day by day, hour by hour, minute by minute, is heartbreaking.

I finally accepted and embraced what Scott was telling me, and it helped. Dave's illness was not the entirety of my life. I did have work. It kept me busy, passed the time and I was surrounded by people who were in better seasons of their lives. My children and grandchildren needed me. I continued to write in my Gratitude Journal and was aware that I was blessed in many ways.

I tried to do everything myself for a long, long, time and finally accepted help. Our church *family* is wonderful. E-mails were sent: "Could you help provide a hot dinner for a family because they are going through difficult times?" It was during the last few weeks of Dave's life, and everything was critical. My family was around all the time, and we didn't cook, but we would have people arrive at our door … *this was so humbling to me.* People would come to the house with full dinners, nothing fancy, but a full meal for us. And these were families struggling with their own issues. There was a single mother with her own kids, and she had worked late that night, and she came up to my fancy neighborhood. I told my daughter, as they walked up to our beautiful home, she must be thinking, "Why is she asking for dinners? She surely has money to just hire somebody." But it wasn't about that. It was about reaching out and helping each other in a very terrible time of need. *Does that make sense?* I kept telling myself, "This isn't forever."

(David) Wade Burge was a great help to his dad at this terrible time and a great help to me. I met Wade when he was about two years old, and he came to live with us a few times and then went back and lived with his mom in Michigan. *I believe God moves people around to be in the right place with the right talents at the right time.* Wade is a perfect example. Several years back he took some nursing classes and was thinking about going into nursing as a career. He had tried different careers, and before committing to a full schedule of nursing studies, he worked in a home for seniors. He became the Activities Director. He always loved doing this for our extended family, and now he was in a job where he had to assist people who weren't able to be mobile on their own. He learned how to lift a patient who was in pain or who couldn't move out of bed. He could move the sheets in such a way as to make this maneuver comfortable for the patient. He was honing specialized skills he would eventually use to bring comfort to his own dad. Wade spent about six weeks with me at the house, and all of his skills were utilized so that his dad would not be hurt. Wade had come to live with us for a couple of years when he worked with his dad in real estate. We couldn't have two Daves, so we used his middle name, Wade, but he'll always be Dave to me. At one time, my Dave had to take fifteen different medicines. They had to be given at different times, and he had tubes that had to be cleaned every day, he required multiple injections, and vials and tubes and needles were all over the place. My wonderfully creative son-in-law, Jeff, realized that a spreadsheet would make the process orderly, and he put together a spreadsheet for me to use. We became a very efficient team! My brother-in-law, Pete, arrived in the last weeks of Dave's life and helped us with physical things that had to be done around the house. It was around Christmas, and decorations had to be taken down and stored, and he knew how to do this. His other brother, Bob, is very good in the financial arena, and he came to town weeks later, after Dave passed, and stayed with me for three days to help me get financial records into shape. My son, Brian, managed the best he could as he was working night shifts and helping care for two children that went back and forth between him and their mother. One thing we could always count on was for Brian to bring his dad red licorice, which Dave loved to eat for as long as I can remember.

I relied on my RED LIPSTICK so many times and in some wacky situations. By the time Dave was anticipating what would be his last Christmas, he was very weak and could barely walk, but he insisted on going shopping to pick out wine for Christmas Eve. We were together in a store that sold all kinds of camping items. When I turned away for a minute, Dave had disappeared. I looked all around this huge store and even had some staff assisting me. We would go up to strangers and ask if they had seen this bald-headed man with a cane and a type of medical bag hanging from his waist. Three bags were collecting the nasty fluids oozing from what appeared to be his mid-section. Yes! Dave was out and about with drains affixed to him; tubes inserted into incisions had been made just for this purpose. He didn't look like your ordinary "man in the street," yet no one had seen him! I was frantic. Where had he gone? He had his cell phone with him, and I dialed the number. He wouldn't always answer me. Sometimes he just forgot how to work the phone. He picked up the call but didn't say anything to me and I started yelling, "If anyone can hear me, please take the phone." Again, *Where is he?* I stepped into the big parking lot to look for him and noticed a wine shop three doors down. I ran to it, and there he was looking around and all innocent. I yelled at him. "What's the big deal?" he asked. I was treating him like a kid, and he didn't like it. He had this cane and he would poke it at me. "Get away." He was like a child in many ways, and I would have loved to have a book that would help caregivers with things like that. Maybe one day, I'll write it.

The Warrior Within

I needed my RLP when I had to interact with Dave's doctors. "Me," a mere mortal, and I went into battle with a physician who is a world famous and respected specialist in pancreatic cancer. Each woman has a Warrior within, and she can push that Warrior forward at will. Remember, the title of this book is "Give Yourself Permission to Live a BIG

Life." Give yourself permission to speak out; speak up for your own interests and for those who need you. Would your Warrior persona be welcome when you speak to your banker about a loan? Might it be necessary when the auto repair guy tries to sell you a bill-of-goods? He assumes he's dealing with a creampuff when, in fact, he's facing a Warrior. Be a Warrior for a cause. Sherrie Gahn, the Principal of Whitney Elementary School, appeared on the Ellen De Generes television show. She has drawn attention to the children and their families in order to raise money to supply help and hope. The goal is to enable the children to have what it takes to stay in school, to learn and to graduate. When that happens, the cycle of poverty can be broken and the future holds great promise. Office Dynamics is a contributor, and Principal Gahn is the Warrior who brought this opportunity to our attention.

I watched Dave repeatedly going into battle against this disease. He put on his suit of armor and submitted to the most demoralizing and debilitating procedures because he was *betting* he could prolong life and that he could stay with me and with our family. This took tremendous courage. And when he finally held up his hands and said, *no more*, I understood. He was exhausted. The battle had been long, and it was his decision to let go. If we had returned to California and to Dr. Isacoff, I feel certain that man would have been able to prolong Dave's life, but it was clear to all of us who loved Dave that his days as a Warrior had come to an end.

Chapter Four

Commit Oneself …
or, as the French say, s'engager

"Be ever engaged, so that whenever the devil calls
he may find you occupied."
—ST. JEROME

Set goals that ignite your passion. Devise plans that enable you to achieve your goals. Follow a plan as though it's a life preserver and you must cling to it. A lot of people don't set goals because it's not as easy as it seems, and it can be very disappointing to fail to achieve desired results. When you set a goal, you've got to be specific and detailed. Your values have to be considered. This is not a small matter. When I started my business, I realized I would be sacrificing time spent with my children. I value family time, and my kids were little. I was willing to sacrifice family time with the children *temporarily* because I knew I had to build a strong foundation for my business. I knew if I did, eventually I could have lots of time to be with my kids. I would have an assistant and be able to say "yes" to time out of the office to attend school activities and the like.

Sacrifice comes in various forms, which may include buying a used car instead of a new car, taking a stay-close-to-home vacation instead of a costly cruise or postponing the remodeling of the kitchen. I don't recall ever setting a goal that did not include sacrifice. Living a BIG Life is synonymous with giving up something for what you're receiving ... exchanging this for that. One thing I refuse to sacrifice is my integrity—my honesty.

I was put into a delicate situation in the early days of starting my business. I could have earned a coveted fee-for-service from a large New York based cosmetics firm until I had this encounter. The CEO didn't show his true colors in my presence, but the administrative assistants told me he was verbally abusive. These efficient women were in tears when they spoke to me in private. When it was time for me to give my view about which skills needed to be developed, this CEO changed the subject completely. He had three assistants working for him, and he wanted me to fire one of them. He kept saying to me, "She's too green, and I need to let her go." I objected. "She is very talented and just needs some training, which is the reason you called me." It was near the end of the business day, and I had to get to the airport, which was about one hour's drive-time away. The conversation was going nowhere, and I finally looked him in the eye and said, "You called me in as the outside expert and I'm telling you, she has potential; she has talent." I was never called back. They didn't pay the balance of what they owed me. I thought, "If that's their work ethic, I don't want to do business with them." I have learned more from being in a tight spot, from barriers and obstacles than I ever learned when everything is rolling along smoothly.

Goals can be big or small. Once you learn the process of setting goals, you can apply that process to all aspects of your life (i.e., personal, professional, financial). If, for example, you want to learn to speak French, you'll make plans to accomplish your goal. You may buy an audio course or attend classes. You'll set aside time to learn and study. If you don't listen to the audio lessons or you rarely attend classes, you won't speak French! You'll have to make a new plan or give up on this aspiration. People who set goals and work diligently to achieve them aren't likely to get caught up in water-cooler or over-the-back-fence gossip. In short, there's no time for unkind chatter and petty jealousies when you're living a BIG Life. *No time for nonsense* is a benefit that may go unnoticed, but it is a benefit of living a BIG Life; *don't you agree?* Are there other unexpected benefits that accrue when you're engaged in a pursuit, involved, occupied or absorbed? Dozens!

Your goal may be as uncomplicated as turning one room in your house into a sewing room. If a shortage of funds keeps you from having that sewing room, should you get a part-time job? Could you buy a table from a second-hand merchandise store or at a yard sale and substitute it to serve in place of shelves that would have otherwise been built by a carpenter? If you take on this project as a do-it-yourself-project, it's likely you'll need far less money to realize your dream. And so it goes! Goals come in all shapes and sizes, and they can be achieved with dispatch or with preparation and patience.

I get my nails done every two weeks and didn't start this until I was older. I'm in front of the public all the time, and it's important that I *stay manicured* and look good, and so my appointment is important. Sometimes, Dave would hear me say I am so busy I don't know when I'm going to get this particular thing done. I'm *slammed* at work. He would tease me. "You always have time for your nail appointment." And I would say, "Of course I do." I'm committed to that nail appointment, and when we are committed, we *part the waters* and make time. So much of what we do or don't do begins with the messages we give to ourselves. *I have time for my nail appointment.*

Now, let's say you are committed to taking a cruise. You saved money to pay for it and you made reservations, but something erupts on a personal or professional level that bumps this dream trip off the front burner. If you give yourself the message that this opportunity will present itself again, then you're in a positive position to *make it happen*. At first I was afraid to put things on a back burner. I found it might be another year or two, but I could commit to something that couldn't be done immediately, and it would be okay.

At about the time Dave was diagnosed with pancreatic cancer, I received a business offer from a high-level Human Resources person in a major corporation. This company does business worldwide, and I was excited at the prospect of working with their most senior executive assistants. I was called early in May 2010, and Dave's health took a deep dive Memorial weekend of 2010. He got worse throughout the summer. I could not give this new client *my all*. I could not be on-site as much as they wanted and could not devote the hours to research in my office as I could have done under normal circumstances. So there I was with a crème de la crème client and could not fully serve their needs because of Dave's illness and my commitment to him. When I was working on-site for this client, *I wasn't always myself.* After all, my husband was in the fight of his life and very, very sick. How could I possibly be 100 percent motivated or excited? How could I possibly focus 100 percent on my audience and my work? Not even the finest of professional speakers are so controlled they can block out all personal problems that fall under the heading of crises. Yet, as a professional speaker, I must get up on stage and deliver the best I can for my participants. And that is what I tried to do, even though some days I was dying inside. I was sick to my stomach having to deal with everything. Often, when I was on-site, I was handling calls that were pertinent to Dave's illness or managing his business finances during my breaks, at lunch time and in the evenings. It was a poignant time in my life; I believe this was the biggest mountain I have ever climbed. I was pulled in one hundred directions at the same time and just managed to keep my head above water.

Thanks to my main contact at this Fortune 100 Company, who was very understanding and patient with me and my situation, the relationship held. She kept her faith in me, and it's not surprising that we became friends.

As of this writing, this client-vendor relationship in not only up and running, but it thrives! The company adopted my Star Achievement Series® curriculum.

I'm such a goal oriented person and think in terms of the big picture and everything that leads up to it. I wake up and tell myself I'm going to accomplish ten specific things today. My style is to be action-oriented, and for as long as I can remember, all was right in my world, and setting goals for me to achieve daily worked well.

When Dave was sick, I could plan what I would do the next day: "I'll do A, B, C and then go home to be with Dave." Nine times out of ten I'd wake up, and something related to Dave's circumstances would be topsy-turvy. I'd get so frustrated. My Pastor said to me, "Have your expectations for what you want to accomplish tomorrow, but don't get your heart set on it. Don't put so much into it that when you get a call and something has happened, you *lose your cool.*"

Clearly some things cannot wait! They must be attended to immediately. And Dave could not wait, should not have had to wait.

I always thought of myself as an observant person and couldn't believe it when I overlooked the fact that Dave was jaundiced. Dave didn't feel well for about five months before he was properly diagnosed. I was shocked that I hadn't noticed during all that time! We just thought he was having stomach problems, and since he had kidney stones when he was younger, this seemed plausible. He went to see numerous doctors and was prescribed one pill or another or an antibiotic. One day he started to scratch himself, first his arms then his legs. He got so itchy he couldn't stand it. Thank God for our gastroenterologist, Dr. Michael Zimmerman. He was determined to discover what was going on. On Memorial Day, Dave had to go to the hospital emergency room because a bile duct had collapsed. We thought, "Dr. Zimmerman will put in a stent and everything will be okay." Two weeks later, they removed the stent and three days later Dave was back in the hospital. We learned that a stent in a bile duct is not like a stent in a heart. There's a heavy concentration of toxins in that part of the body and Dave had to have the stent changed (in the hospital) every six weeks or thereabouts for two years.

Prolific author and motivational speaker Napoleon Hill wrote, "When defeat comes, accept it as a signal that your plans are not sound, rebuild those plans, and set sail once more toward your coveted goal."

Mr. Hill doesn't suggest that a goal isn't sound but rather that the method for attaining it needs to be adjusted. I suspect Mr. Hill, who died in 1970, knew a good deal about living a BIG Life!

At the writing of this book and sixteen months after Dave's passing, I am at another crossroad. On January 4, 2012, I had made it through the first year since Dave's passing. All I heard people talk about was that first year after you lose a person you love: the first holiday, the first birthday, the first anniversary. And I had made it. I was jubilant the first three weeks of January. I had goals pouring out of my head. I had post-it notes hanging everywhere as that is how I capture my immediate, good ideas. And then, bam, the *unexpected* hit me again but through my children and challenges they were facing—this happened with both adult children within three weeks of each other. *Oh no, are you serious? Can't I ever get a break?* Once again, I am reminded that my goals and plans don't always fall into place and don't come in a neat, tidy little box. It is months now that we have been moving through some tough stuff, and I keep telling my daughter and son, "Thank goodness I have experience from your dad's situation." While the situations are very different, I find I need the same skills I needed to assist Dave. I need to find the right people who can help us navigate. I know to ask lots of questions and get facts and details. I document every phone call with the date and time and jot down what I was told. I know how to direct my children as they are now on their journey of life as adults. The hope is that we accumulate skills and knowledge along the way that help us with the next big adventure. I am still writing in my Gratitude Journal and find several things each day for which to thank God. When we lead a BIG Life, we never stop being friends, parents, siblings, neighbors, leaders, co-workers, grandparents, uncles, aunts or community supporters.

As Albert Einstein wrote, "Learn from yesterday, live for today, hope for tomorrow. The important thing is not to stop questioning." And I'm tempted to add: The important thing is not to stop believing.

Chapter Five

Create What You Want

"A man is a success if he gets up in the morning and gets to bed at night, and in between he does what he wants to do."
—BOB DYLAN

I almost closed the door of my company on three different occasions. I wasn't an employee working for someone else, and we relied on my income. *How am I going to pull this out?* I always went back to bare-bones operations. There are many little ways you can save money, and we utilized all of them.

The first time I almost closed my doors was two and one-half years after starting Office Dynamics. We were living in Virginia Beach at the time, and Dave got a good promotion that resulted in our relocation to Lansing, Michigan. When we moved, I was virtually back to square one. 90 percent of the business I had was with local companies in the Virginia Beach Hampton Roads area. Those clients could not afford to fly me back and forth to train their administrative professionals. It took an entire year for me to build business in my new *neighborhood*. At the same time, I started to advertise in training publications that were widely circulated and landed my first large corporate client: Caterpillar Inc., in Peoria, Illinois. I was so excited; I thought I had died and gone to heaven. This was what I wanted! Ronnie (Veronica) was the wonderful person at Caterpillar who hired me and kept me coming back. I was still teaching at Caterpillar five years later because management witnessed first-hand the value of the training. The company's administrative assistants made it possible for the executives they supported to be more productive. Everyone was happy!

I created what I wanted … and I wanted more. Eventually I had clients across the United States and in Jamaica. I was meeting thousands of people and going into all kinds of business environments. I continued to learn, too, and to grow my business.

Even after that success, there were bumps in the road. The third and final time I almost closed the company happened in 2001. We had just moved to Las Vegas, and the economy was down. Then the September 11 attacks changed air travel forever. My business requires me to speak to administrative assistants on-site. After the attacks, I was paralyzed with a fear of flying. At the time, Dave was semi-retired, and he needed to generate full-time-work income. I wasn't going to give up what I had worked for ten years to acquire. As it happened, Dave was growing bored with semi-retirement and was ready to step back into something more stimulating. For both of us, I needed to overcome my fears and keep my business going. And that is exactly what I did.

When I was a child in Catholic School, I wanted to be a nun. I had wanted to be a teacher, and my teachers were nuns. One Christmas, my parents bought me a nun's outfit. I would come home from school every day and put on my nun's outfit. *I had a classroom in the attic and I had my imaginary students and I would teach.* When I got to high school, I discovered that nuns don't marry. I was boy-crazy, and I quickly trashed my plan to become a nun. But I hung onto my desire for teaching, learning and collecting words!

For some reason, the word *evolve* kept jumping into my head as I struggled to buoy my business. Evolve means to develop gradually. I had to temper my energy with just the right dash of enthusiasm and planning and the right dash of accepting gradual development. (In the very beginning it took nine months to earn some money, and the first check was only $250.) If I hadn't been realistic about going slow, I might have gotten discouraged or at the least have been disappointed, and that would not take me where I had wanted to go. I wanted to save my business!

The word *evolve* makes me think of something else, too. Dave's career took us many places to live: Minneapolis, Minnesota; Asheville, North Carolina; Memphis, Tennessee; Virginia Beach, Virginia; and Lansing, Michigan. Prior to this, I had always lived in Cleveland. When we left Cleveland, Dave didn't have a job. Brian was about two years old, and Lauren was three and one-half years old. We just knew we had to change our life. We rented a small U-Haul truck, packed our possessions into it and went to live with Dave's parents in South Carolina, believing that

Dave would find a job of some sort. His folks lived in this tiny, tiny, town called Greenwood, and I knew I wasn't going to stay there. Every day we would drive an hour into a bigger town, and Dave would hunt for a job. We'd look in the paper and go out day after day after day and still "no job." *Where were we going to live?* Then, on a Friday afternoon, I'll never forget it, there was one company in this little business complex, and we said, "All right, one more stop." The *"one more"* changed Dave's career and our lives. That's how he got into outdoor advertising and started us onto a wonderful journey and his incredible career that opened our eyes to so many things.

After leaving Cleveland, I met so many people and worked in different environments and realized people are all different. *My way isn't the only way.* I evolve—adjust, progress, grow and change. I have learned a myriad of new things. I've been *tested* many times and proved to myself … *yes, I can!* My self-confidence swelled. And each challenge met prepared me for the next.

Sometimes we don't see something until we look back after decades pass. Little did I know as a child that the stage was being set for me to teach. I am teaching adults, and most of our focus is on the career I love. If I hadn't been an assistant and hadn't worked in all those places, I couldn't do what I do today. God had me in training. And now I feel as though the understanding I have gained by living for more than half a century and especially by coming through the trials of these past years has prepared me to speak to women from all walks of life. Once again, the stage was being set. I want to reach more women in addition to working with administrative career professionals. I believe in women. I want to help empower women. Women are very strong, and yet we are fragile. I would love for women to improve the quality of their work-life and experience more joy. I want to help them reduce stress, and, if I can, help them be prepared for what might occur. I'm a firm believer in being pro-active. For example, self-esteem is a huge issue for women, and it often fluctuates based upon what people say to women. When the manager comes into the office and *badgers* or a spouse comes into the room and announces, "You are stupid," instead of defending their positions, women question themselves. This response is usually born of old ways of thinking. Today's woman can self-manage—it's easy to do once you're introduced to the concept and have the tools for the task. I use self-management tools all the time.

Dr. George Pransky introduced me to self-management. I met George some years ago when Dave was working for Adams Outdoor Advertising. George Pransky was hired by Adams Outdoor to work with high-level management. Twice a year, Pransky led special retreats for these managers and their spouses. One thing I learned is to not permit my emotions to overpower my intellect. I may be involved in something throughout the day that I find distressing. I can choose to say, "Okay, I'm frustrated with this situation (or person), but I'm choosing to take a different path. I want to go into problem-solving mode." Or I may say, "I'll address this with that person tomorrow." Or I may be attending a meeting, and a participant is upsetting me. I can stop and look at that individual and find something positive about the person (e.g., she gives me her undivided attention). Focusing on something positive is a *good thing* to do. Thinking about good things helps reduce tension. Self-management tools guide me to look at the big picture. Sometimes we get so caught up with little things we let them swell. Finally, months after Dave passed, I decided to remodel some rooms in my house, including the kitchen. The first week of remodeling my house was not going well. I would come home after an intense day at the office, and there would be a mess in my kitchen, or it was immediately evident that someone had done something really stupid. *How could you do this to my house? You ruined my kitchen cabinets!* I was so upset that one night I telephoned my neighbor. "I have to talk to you because I'm so angry right now." And I went through this for about one week until I realized, "This isn't doing any good." All my nights were *thrown-off*. SELF-TALK came to my rescue. *I don't have to put this pressure on myself. Even though I wanted it done by a certain date, when it gets done, it will get done.* My step-mom was very helpful. "You have more important things to focus on than the disaster they created in your house." It was a big thing, but it was a little thing. It had been going on for weeks. It was interrupting my life. I used self-management tools and *leaned into what was happening. Go with the flow. Okay, that happened today. When are they going to fix it?* Then I went ahead and did what I was going to do. I went to the gym or went out to meet my kids or to walk the dogs. This process continued for five months. In order to Live a BIG Life we have to rise up. That's where that spiritual connection comes in. If we get back in tune with ourselves, then all of a sudden the burdens of day-to-day *issues* just shrink. As a matter of fact, they look downright small. In the big picture they're not that important. I recently read an article in "Success Magazine," one of my favorite magazines. It was about a man who survived a heart attack and how he completely shifted his priorities. Without a reminder, it's easy to get caught up in the nitty-gritty. This morning, I had so many e-mails and phone calls, and everyone wanted everything NOW. If we self-manage, step back, take a breath and get in touch with what is really important in our life, it's such a relief. We can operate at a higher level; we can be more creative. It's all a part of living a BIG Life.

There are days when my mind is filled with worry. (I call it *a worry-mind*.) We worry and worry about something coming, and often it never arrives. But even if it does arrive, worry isn't going to change the outcome. If, for example, I worry that cash flow will be slow and Accounts Receivable may exceed thirty days, I worry about paying my bills. I stop and think that in spite of what I read in the newspapers about the dismal state of the economy, this isn't a likely scenario. I know my clients well, and none have given me a reason to think they'll be late. If I find that the worry goes on, I consider my options. (Another self-management tool is to deal with worry that goes on and on and on. This is not to say you must nip it in the bud, but do pay attention to how long worry has dogged you.) If the Accounts Receivable ledger tells me I'm short of funds at the end of the Quarter, I'll do A, B or C. If no one pays late, it's a moot point. Either way, don't set a place at your table for a worry-mind when you're intent on living a BIG Life.

You may already use many of these strategies but don't think of them as self-management tools. You'll pick up suggestions from friends and colleagues that deserve that label too. And you'll read books and articles that expound on solutions. Solutions are often dependent on self-management. Andy Stanley discusses self-management in his book, "The Principle of the Path: How to Get from Where You Are to Where You Want to Be." Take what you find and make it your own. Shape it and customize it until you're the best you can be and can create what you want.

My mom always taught me no matter what I do, it should be the best I can do. If you sew a button, do it the best you can. *Use a double thread. Start sewing on the wrong side of the fabric. Wind the double thread around under the button to make a shank. Secure the thread well before you snip off the excess.* If you clean your house, give it your best effort. *Check cleaning supplies. Replace missing supplies. Determine time needed for each room. And this is just for starters.* Of course we don't love everything we do, but whatever we do, we must offer up our best. My mother imbued me with this philosophy, and I tried to teach it to my children. In addition to the short-term rewards (e.g., approval), you are being prepared for your future. No one should diminish any role she is playing today. Even if you aspire to doing "something more" ... do your best work now.

My sister Janet is our family's Lucille Ball. She makes us see the funny side of life. But Janet is also a creative and talented decorator. She never studied home or industrial decorating and doesn't make her living as a decorator, but I love it when she helps me rearrange furniture or pictures on the walls in my home. Would she evolve and use her God-given talents *to the hilt* if she expanded her circle and moved away from Cleveland? I think not. Janet is a happy person who uses her amazing talents in a way that "works" for her. I expanded my circle after leaving home, and in so doing, I grew; you don't have to leave home to expand your circle. But in order to Live a BIG Life you must expand your circle. Volunteer at polling places for Election Day, help teach children how to read or take a part-time job performing tasks that are new to you. When you expand your circle, opportunity pays a call, and you grow whether you planned on it or not.

When we lived in Michigan, Dave had a wonderful career until it ended abruptly. With the arrival of new top management ... the hand-writing was on the wall, and then in one day, my life shifted. We lost the nice company car, benefits and friendships; we lost (almost) everything. The good news was that Dave had a good severance package. That sustained us until the kids got out of high school. I didn't want to stay in Lansing, Michigan, even though I had loved it. I had loved it because of what Dave's position made possible for us. He was the General Manager. We did wonderful things with the company, but now that was gone. I thought, "We have to be somewhere else," but I didn't know where. Prior to Dave's dismissal, I had speaking engagements in Las Vegas. When I first saw the desert, I had thought that it might be nice to live somewhere where you have an abundance of sunshine year-round and aren't confined due to freezing temperatures and snowstorms. It was a passing thought, but when a move seemed like a good thing to do, Las Vegas jumped back onto my radar screen. Dave and I made the decision to come here, and my dad asked, "Why would you do that? You have a wonderful home in Michigan." We did, but I wanted to experience something different. I always felt that if something didn't work out, we could go back. And I also asked myself, "What am I missing?" Many people miss things because they're afraid to try something new. They don't permit themselves to entertain those thoughts. Dave and I and the children came to Las Vegas filled with excitement and enthusiasm for what lay ahead. We had no idea that Dave's health would soon be dramatically compromised. That is significant because if we had been living in Michigan, we wouldn't have been able to fly to California every two weeks. Thank God we were in Nevada and could get to UCLA and meet Dr. Reber and Dr. Isacoff. These doctors gave Dave the help he needed to prolong his life. We made that "every two week" trip for seven consecutive months. And Dave lived longer than he would have if we had still lived in Michigan.

Chapter Six

F-O-C-U-S

"The shorter way to do many things is
to do one thing at a time."
—MOZART

I would add to Mozart's observation that it's also the only way to do many things and to have each thing turn out as good as can be. When we don't focus, we can't do a good job and we're not as creative. Our best *thought process* isn't engaged. We become stressed. If I have five things going on in my head right now, I feel overwhelmed. I feel stressed. I think, "OMG how can I get this done?" When I'm focused, fully focused like I am right now writing this chapter, or focused on something else that I'm doing—I'm so much more at peace. I'm engaged. *I'm in the moment.*

Today's technology can seduce us. If we don't pay attention, it's easy to fall prey. Here's an illustration: I travel all the time. I eat dinner alone 90 percent of the time. I don't mind; I get to observe everyone in the dining area. One night I was in Albuquerque, New Mexico, and I saw a mother and young child having dinner together, and she did not talk to that little child the entire time I was there. She was busy texting on her phone, and this poor little child sat there and pushed her fork around on the plate. I wanted to shout, "Why aren't you focused? Why aren't you in the moment?" Are we that blind that we're actively missing out on *human moments*? I have a real issue with this … you are cheating yourself. You will never ever get that moment back. When you're older and look back on life, do you think you're going to say, "I wish I would have spent more time texting"? You're going to say, "What a fool I was. My child is grown up now, and I'll never get that back into my life."

Towards the end of Dave's battle with pancreatic cancer, I would often ask myself, "Is Dave going to be here a month from now?" Maybe he would survive for three months, six months or even one year. I felt so *stressed* I knew I had to stop that thought process. My dad was a big help. He would remind me, "Just focus on today. That is the best you can do."

Without a doubt, this period of time called for RLP … Red Lipstick Power (I write about this in Chapter Two). When I hear the words, "Red Lipstick ON!" … I tell myself, "Pull back from the abyss and focus." If you need a quick way to remind yourself to focus, you may want to use this reminder to achieve your goal. Raise your voice and declare, "Red Lipstick ON!"

A circus juggler will focus and yet be able to keep many balls in the air at once. That entertainer is dramatically aware of the difference between FOCUS and JUGGLE. The juggler will focus for an instant on the balls she has in hand. She will make a quick move to release those balls and then for an instant focus on the next balls she has in hand. The juggling process is repeated.

To multi-task is to do many things at once. You may be speaking on the phone, folding the laundry and keeping an eye on a kitchen timer so you don't over-cook the meatloaf. I'm focused on writing this chapter, but in my peripheral vision I know there are about a dozen things I must address. I'll move them around just like a juggler and keep my focus on what's happening right now. Some people express this as *living in the moment*. The juggler lives in the second!

People aren't born jugglers. It is essential to practice in order to learn juggling. People who are serious about becoming expert jugglers report that eventually they are fit, strong, patient and relaxed masters of self-discipline. I expect they're tireless too; they don't get weary because they're not worrying about what's coming next. When "next" arrives, they deal with it.

Chapter Seven

Riding the Waves of Change

"A man who misses his opportunity, and a monkey who misses his branch, cannot be saved."
—HINDU PROVERB

Sometimes change is good, and sometimes it's not so good. But when we don't recognize that it comes complete with opportunity, we can be like the monkey who misses his branch!

Years ago when Dave and I decided to move to Las Vegas, my dad saw danger lurking in the shadows. He focused on what could go wrong: we could sell our house, move far away to Las Vegas and be unhappy. But I saw opportunity. I wanted to live somewhere really different in our country, and Vegas and the desert was quite different. Since I embrace sunshine like food for my soul, I knew it was the place to move to. At that time, Vegas was a growing, booming town. It seems I have being a risk-taker in my blood, and I thought that if we did not like it, we could always move back to the Midwest, but I knew I would not know until I tried it. Las Vegas is also near California, so we could venture off to the ocean, beautiful San Diego, or wine country.

Danger and opportunity are kissing cousins who frequently dance on your doorstep in times of change. If you let danger take the lead, there's no telling what you'll miss. A woman who lives a BIG Life is willing to explore opportunities.

When I first started Office Dynamics and began to travel, Dave would say to me, "I thought I married this Italian woman, a secretary who was going to stay home and cook pasta every night." Well, you know what? I'm not that person anymore. I was, but I'm not and I can't go back.

When we change, we may scare people. I don't think I could have moved more slowly to permit Dave to adjust to the change. I had to forge ahead because I was serious about making my business successful. You're the one who must hold fast and not be frightened by change. If ever there is a good time to think about "living in the moment," a time of change is it. When I do live in the moment, I don't feel anxious or drain my energy.

I've heard so many women in my workshops talk about what happens when they are more assertive; they're greeted by harsh tones and asked, "Why are you acting this way?" It's as though this adult person has transgressed because she has an opinion and is able to speak up. Many of the women tell me they go back to being quiet. Perhaps it's the path of least resistance, but it's not a path that leads to living a BIG Life. People who discourage you from riding the waves of change may be enriched by the *new you*, but they can't see that far ahead. It takes courage to persevere, but nothing prevents you from having a parachute too. My parachute is made up of *I-could-always-do* things. For example, I could always go back to work as an executive assistant.

There are all kinds of change. Children become adults and move away. They go to college or marry. Your relationships change. Parents age to a point where they are not as independent as when they were younger. You devote time to satisfying their needs. You get a promotion, and the job description is different. Your office staff changes. You lose fifty pounds and don't recognize yourself in the mirror. You earn a university degree, and you become the teacher and are no longer the student.

Our bodies change as we age. Can we do something to avoid the so-called ravages of the years? Yes! Pay attention to the Wellness Pillar in Chapter Two. If you do this all your life, you're in an enviable position, but if this is new to you, don't despair. It's never too late to begin to take good care of yourself. According to experts, physical exercise can be added to your regimen at virtually any age and your body will respond favorably. You may never compete in marathons, but you may astound yourself by how you can change for the better.

I'd rather live a short, full BIG Life than a long, small life. Every time I "see" some way to make myself a better person, I give it a try. That doesn't mean I'm always right or that I don't make mistakes. I learn from my mistakes, and that experience helps me move forward.

Letting Go of Old Things

Years ago we had our Office Dynamics office in a house in a residential neighborhood. It came complete with a swimming pool and a lovely back yard where palm trees grew. I never wanted to put my office in that house. It was Dave's idea to do it, and he owned the house. At one time it was occupied by renters, but when it was vacant Dave urged me to make this move. "Stay five years," he suggested. I didn't want to stay for five minutes! But move we did. My office windows looked out onto a beautiful lawn and pool. In time I grew to love that wonderful house. When Dave died, Office Dynamics and I had to vacate the premises (five years later, as he had said). In April 2011, we moved into commercial real estate offices, and I felt the full impact of the financial responsibility. The beautiful yard was replaced by a cement wall! Nevertheless, sometimes we have to move on and let go of old things so we can live that BIG Life. Today, I'm pleased with our offices and location, and, happily, business is in a growth spurt and I foresee the need for more space and new offices. When everything feels strange because it's new and different, I recognize I'm in LIMBO. The LIMBO I think of is not the Caribbean dance but the place of confinement that is transitory; it is neither here nor there. This serves as my comfort zone. I understand now that it's okay to just hang out in LIMBO. *I don't know where this is going to lead. I don't know what GOD has in mind, but all I have to do is take one step forward: the next step.* I can do that. You can do that too. Later on, when you look back at what transpired, you may recognize how all the pieces came together to lead you where you are today. LIMBO is a comfortable place to be for a short time. The action-oriented woman who lives a BIG Life won't linger too long.

Chapter Eight

A Gratitude Journal on my Nightstand

"The more you recognize and express
gratitude for the things you have, the more things
you will have to express gratitude for."
—ZIG ZIGLAR

When they closed up Dave after three hours of surgery and came to tell me he had pancreatic cancer that had spread to the superior mesenteric vein (a major vein) and they couldn't do anything for him, I felt like I was in a *Black Hole*. I felt like I was falling into this very, very deep hole with no bottom, and I wondered to whom I could turn. My sister, Gina, gave me a Gratitude Journal. It is entitled "The Secret," and it was very popular at the time. I found that by writing (not just by thinking but by writing), my list just grew and grew. It was amazing to see how many things for which I was grateful. We stayed at this one particular hotel all the time when we had to go to California for Dave's treatments and surgeries, and I thought, "I'm just grateful that I can stay in this nice hotel and that I can afford to stay in a nice hotel even though we're here for a horrible, horrible reason. I'm so grateful we can afford to have a nice dinner, and I'm grateful for these wonderful surgeons. I'm grateful that I can walk over to the doctor's office."

When I'm not reading or writing in my Journal, I leave it next to my bed so that I see it before I turn out the lights. No matter how weary I may be, I can always manage to make a few notes. I don't know if it's true, but I've heard that women tend to focus more on what they didn't accomplish than what they did accomplish. By the end of a day, you can find at least one thing for which to be grateful. (I invite you to look at some of my Journal entries that have been reprinted in the back of this book.)

One of the things Dave and I were especially grateful for was the *outpouring from around the world*. Dave received over three hundred cards. He didn't know these people, but they knew about him because I spoke about him and wrote about him. I have a sixty-page stapled memoir book that Jasmine assembled. It's made up of e-mail messages from people around the world. I don't recognize the names of all the senders, but each one touched us deeply.

Dave would be in bed and I would sit there with my computer and read these messages coming from around the world. We would both be in tears. But that's what helped us. There is support. There is strength. Every day we would get these cards. I cannot forget this. They held me up!

Even now, I read through old notes I had written, and it reminds me of how blessed I have been in spite of all the heartache, turmoil and flurry of my life. I am blessed every day. Women are juggling so many things and have a laundry list of "must do today" that we just can't accomplish it all. Focusing on one little thing we accomplished or what makes us feel grateful today helps us Live a BIG Life.

Journaling is also known to help us manage stress and increases our self-esteem. It feels good to get your thoughts onto paper and then move on.

(You can purchase your Live a BIG Life Gratitude Journal at www.JoanBurgeBIGLife.com)

Chapter Nine

You Are Always On Stage

"A well-dressed woman, even though her purse is painfully empty, can conquer the world."
—LOUISE BROOKS

I never leave the house looking like something the proverbial cat dragged in. Think of it! Ugh! I always want to be in position to conquer the world. What do you think about the young woman who shows up at a law firm to interview for a job and is dressed as though she is going to the neighborhood playground? She is wearing baggy and faded pants, her nail polish is chipped, her hair is stuffed under a cap and well ... you get the picture. Even if her educational credentials are impressive, she isn't likely to win a job offer.

On the way to living a BIG Life, you want to gain the respect of others. Women need to take off the blinders ... we're in a newer era of casualness, but from my work with women in the workplace I see first-hand how many of them use questionable judgment regarding just how "casual" they should be.

Once, high-level executives at a certain large corporation had expressed interest in working with me. I was to come in and work with their executive assistants. They wanted to empower their assistants; they wanted this profession to be viewed as a true profession within their organization. It was wonderful. I loved it that they were such visionaries. So I put on my business uniform. I like to wear my sweatpants, and I like to wear my shorts and tennis shoes, but there's a time and a place for all of that. I have all those different *uniforms* to suit each occasion. So I was going in for my first interview within the big prestigious organization, and there were to be some top executives sitting there. It was 2010, and I was going into a workplace where "casual" was an accepted way of life. My hair, nails and make-up were attended to with care, and I wore a skirt suit, nice jewelry and carried a handbag that coordinated with my high-heel shoes. When I walked into the room, the executive at the head of the conference table greeted me and motioned me to sit down. She lifted the phone to call another executive who was going to participate in our meeting and finally called a third to come and join us. When that person came to the conference room door, I stood up and said, "Hi, I'm Joan Burge." And he said, "Well, I can see this is going to be a real game changer." He obviously came to that conclusion based, in part, upon how I was dressed.

It takes courage to do what is right in your opinion. Just because everyone is doing something else you need not relinquish your convictions. It takes courage to Live a BIG Life.

There's a child inside of each of us who is screaming to get out. As we age, people are telling us what to think, what to do—don't do this, don't do this—and it starts to color our vision. We're no longer playful; we push our creativity to the *back of the bus,* and this frequently makes us feel tired. Oh yes, we go out to dinner once in a while and we go mountain climbing and on a cruise, but then we're back to the drudgery. It was a joy to watch people who fit this description change before our eyes. Some of the attendees to one Office Dynamics convention didn't know how to pretend. We used to pretend when we were kids and didn't have all these technological gimmicks to entertain us. It was our Gala Dinner evening, and the attendees were wearing beautiful cocktail dresses or gowns, their fancy heels or dress shoes and their hair and make-up were just so, but when a red carpet was rolled out for them, many didn't know how to walk on it!

When they started to get the hang of it, some of them strutted and twirled and had their pictures taken, posing while making extravagant gestures, and it was wonderful. They told on-lookers about their designers (e.g., Tar-get), and you could feel the energy rise in the room. Smiles were abundant and people bonded because we created an environment for attendees that gave them permission to have fun. We don't often get permission to have fun, let down our hair and be a kid. We're adults and, "Oh my shame on you, you're acting like a kid! You shouldn't do that." Well you know what? At sixty years old I will still go to a rock concert with Jasmine and my adult kids because they're more fun to hang out with than many people my age.

Good manners, enthusiasm, joy and energy and *all that jazz* are part of your presentation. Can you name someone who you associate with smiles and warmth? As soon as you think of this person, you probably feel good.

I feel good when flight attendants comment on my appearance. As a very frequent flyer, there's no doubt many have seen me over and over and over again. "Clean, neat, matching handbag and shoes; you're an inspiration!" Compliments are tiny gems to have and to hold, and acting as an inspiration to others is a bonus. When I take my car to the car wash in my Las Vegas neighborhood, one attendant tells me, "You always look so great." That's a confidence booster if ever there was one.

Chapter Ten

My Spirituality & God's Grace

"Faith is like the radar that sees through the fog."
—CORRIE TEN BOOM 1892 -1983

OR ... "Through many dangers, toils and snares, I have already
come; 'Tis grace has brought me safe thus far,
And grace will lead me home."
—JOHN NEWTON, ENGLISH COMPOSER 1725 - 1807

I don't need to be in church to have a relationship with God. I can be talking to God when I'm walking my dogs or when I'm hiking in the mountains. It grounds me to have this relationship. It brings me back to what is truly important. I feel the spirit within me, and when Dave was so sick and we were constantly in and out of hospitals, my spirituality helped me see the big picture of life and enabled me to put things into perspective.

I liked my mother-in-law. She was ninety years old when she died, and her name was Joan (Hogan) Burge. As a matter of fact, my sister-in-law who lives in Ohio is Joan Burge, too. Since my mother suffered for so many years with depression, it may have been predictable that I would become close to my mother-in-law. My family was more huggy-kissy than Dave's family. My mother-in-law was kind, gentle, and tough and strong. I remember calling from a hotel when I was far from home and asking her about something that was going on with my teenage kids. I was very upset and she said to me, "Oh honey, *don't worry. It all comes out in the wash*." And I asked, "How could you say that? I'm a nervous wreck." She realized whatever way it goes, it goes. So don't overstress. In her own way, she shoved me out of my worry-mode by giving me some encouragement. I have a friend who is fond of saying, "Let go and let God." My belief in God's Grace made it easier for me to accept that *it would all come out in the wash*. Joan Hogan Burge was also telling me to be patient. I trusted her judgment and relaxed.

I prayed and prayed the night Hurricane Floyd was en route to Virginia Beach, VA. It was 1999 and my daughter, Lauren, and I were in Virginia Beach waiting for 125 Office Dynamics Conference for Administrative Excellence attendees to arrive. Women were coming from all over the country, and bad storms were brewing in Florida. The city of Virginia Beach was our host site, and the city fathers (in this case a city mother, too, the mayor who was to be our opening speaker) wanted to show off their tourist area by the ocean with the boardwalks, shops, restaurants and night life. Naturally the hotel we were staying in was built on ocean front property. Lauren, who was working as my assistant in the small office I maintained in Michigan where we lived, was my staff support, and we had a large team of assistants from the host site that would help with all aspects of the conference. Lauren and I arrived on Monday. Early Tuesday the weather report featured Floyd, which was reported to be trekking up the coast heading for Virginia Beach and due to arrive on Thursday, which was the opening day of our conference. I telephoned Dave. "The President announced a State of Emergency for Virginia Beach!" I was petrified. Dave kept telling me that I could handle it and that I was in good hands with the mayor and the city emergency team. I was feeling anxious about what was to come. I felt responsible for the attendees and their safety. I worried about Lauren and me too. Safety was my number one concern. As a business woman, I realized that the big bills for this event had to be paid, and if the conference was cancelled, monies would have to be refunded. I was definitely in a pickle!

By Wednesday, all our attendees had arrived. They were excited about being there for the conference and for the hurricane. That surprised me! Apparently the husbands who urged them to come home and the employers who voiced concerns didn't dampen the enthusiasm of the women who had assembled. I vividly remember standing in a small meeting room with the attendees telling them what to do should the hurricane hit during the night. To prepare everyone, I kept thinking about a philosophy I had been teaching assistants for years in which four main components were critical for Star Achieving success. I mentioned these early in this book. They are skill, attitude, teamwork and strategy. In the skills category, we needed excellent communication, time management and organizational skills. We definitely needed to maintain a positive attitude and stare Hurricane Floyd in the face. We absolutely had to work as a team. We were in this together, and there was no turning back at this late hour. We had to have a plan—a strategy. Everyone knew where to go if the hotel had to be evacuated. Everyone knew how to cooperate to make the most of the flashlights the hotel staff distributed. Since the residents of the city had been buying flashlights, batteries and provisions from the moment Floyd was announced, the hotel staff couldn't provide each of us with a light, but with a "buddy system" in place, everyone would have the light needed to move down the corridors without mishap. By the time Lauren and I went to our room, she wanted some sleep. I could not sleep, but I could pray, and I did over and over again.

I love to tell the story of this event because although I was stretched to my mental and physical limits, great numbers of attendees told me this was the best conference they ever attended! Spirits were high. Women waved streamers, and the feelings of camaraderie shot throughout the gathering as we got ready to go home. I'll never forget the leadership qualities the mayor displayed. She stood about 4' 11" but she showed BIG courage and obviously had BIG self-confidence, and I'd wager that she lives a BIG Life.

I have a long list of what-not-to-do when I host a conference, and it all sprang from this experience. Today we host about 400 administrative professionals who come from all over the world to attend this Office Dynamics event. We have a large team who makes this event run like a fine-tuned well-oiled machine.

As a final note, I should mention I suffered greatly after I returned to the safety of my home, my husband and my children. A few weeks later, I felt so anxious I couldn't be away from my family. I did not want to go anywhere near the ocean or a lake or water! I went for some massage therapy, and I cried like a baby during the massage, releasing everything that had built up in me during the Hurricane Floyd ordeal. This was the first time I had heard about post-traumatic stress symptoms gripping people after involvement in a serious accident or at war time. Apparently, I had just been introduced to PTS.

Heaven-sent Angels

I should not write another word until I take a moment to salute my ANGELS FROM HEAVEN. I could not have sustained the continuity of my business during Dave's battle with pancreatic cancer without Jasmine Freeman. She is a woman of courage and compassion, and when she came to work with me and for Office Dynamics, Ltd., many years ago, we had no idea that she would play a role that was and is central to the company's success. She goes way beyond day-to-day expectations in her capacity as Chief Executive Assistant and adds immeasurably to my peace of mind. Then Michele Busch walked through our door. How fortunate we were on the day that Jasmine interviewed her at the local Coffee Bean cafe and recommended that I take the time to interview her at my office. Hired! She is the vibrant person that people meet when they call our Las Vegas office or walk through our front door, and she is a detail-oriented person who digs into projects with enthusiasm.

My sister, Gina DeGirolamo, has been by my side since Dave was diagnosed with pancreatic cancer. Gina is California based and has had a long career in television. She has a desk at our Office Dynamics address and drives to Las Vegas several times a year to work at that desk. Gina is the woman behind our four websites and all key visual projects (e.g., on-screen presentations at conferences, video for the Internet), but she was with Dave during many of his hospital visits. She was his dinner companion and driver and shoulder to cry on when I couldn't be there for the radiation and chemotherapy appointments. And sometimes, even when I was there, Gina was our driver, our dinner companion and our shoulder to cry on. I could forgo sleep when Dave needed me, but it was essential that I maintained business. So on occasions I was out of

Nevada when Dave had to be in California for treatments, Gina was his *California angel* so to speak.

Nancy Fraze is an angel too. It was serendipitous the way our paths crossed. Our relationship went from a spontaneous "May I join you for lunch?" while I was speaking at Chevron Corporation in California to Nancy writing extensively for Office Dynamics and my using a poem she wrote in 1995 for Dave's Celebration of Life in 2011 (see *And Now The Warrior Returns Home* in the back of the book).

I've mentioned Stephanie Roxbury elsewhere in this book. Dave hired her to assist with accounting and record keeping when he was already ill. She was primed and ready to assist me when I was completely in the dark about so many aspects of Dave's businesses, and she did it and does it all with composure and competency.

There you have it: My Roster of Angels from Heaven:

Jasmine Freeman

Michele Busch

Gina DeGirolamo

Stephanie Roxbury

Nancy Fraze

I thank you all.

Chapter Eleven

Look at Life With a Question Mark ... Not a Period

"An optimist may see a light where there is none,
but why must a pessimist always run to blow it out?"
—RENE DESCARTES 1831 - 1901

Dave and I moved to Asheville, and I didn't like it. I was a big city girl, and there we were in the hills, and I couldn't understand what people were saying. I thought someone was saying "pen," and he was saying "pin." People went swimming in a lake, and I was accustomed to a swimming pool and on and on. I'll just give you the short version. After six months in Asheville, I loved it.

We had been renting a house, and then we decided to buy a house. We set a budget and went shopping. We saw a house up on a hill that I loved, but it was about $15,000 too much. Dave and I were going through a period of debt. I don't mind saying that we struggled. We had both been divorced. Now I could have said, "We can't get that house. Not only is it over our price but we have a horrible credit record." But that's not what I said. I didn't put a period on the possibility. That would mean it was closed, ended and kaput. Instead, I thought, "Dave has a terrific job, and prior to the recent past we had good credit." I went to visit three or four bankers and explained that Dave lost his job just once. At the time, it wasn't acceptable like today when so many people have lost their jobs. I kept telling myself, "Surely some bank in this town is going to give me a loan." I just had to find it. Finally, I found a man who was willing to speak with us. We had to complete lots of paperwork, but we were approved for a mortgage and we loved living in that house. Every day it's likely you have opportunities to supply a *period* to something that confronts you. A period is a full stop. I know that question marks help me to Live a BIG Life.

If you wake up and are having a bad day and have many appointments, pull out that question mark and ask, "How can I make this day more pleasurable, or how can I take some of the stress off myself?" I might promise myself time for a bubble bath at the end of the day. I'll read a favorite magazine while I soak. The very thought of *me time* just ahead can make this day that is filled with so many appointments more agreeable. *Whoosh*, my attitude changes and everything is easier.

Even when a question mark is in place, an answer may be nowhere in sight. It may come to me when I'm driving down the street. It may come to me when I'm putting on my make-up next Tuesday, but I have to have that question mark first. Why would my or your subconscious ponder the question if there's no question? The flip side of this behavior is that sometimes you must let go. It is time to STOP. For one thing, the urgency of a situation can make it impossible to wait. Just don't be too quick to hit the brakes!

Time To Move On

I coached a woman who had good reason to feel aggrieved. Her husband had left her. Her father had gotten sick. She had been caring for him, and he died. She was holding on to her "down" feelings too long, and it was affecting her job. She had to deal with her grief and depression, but it was clear that her self-confidence was shattered. After four months of management extending special consideration to her, I was called in to work with her and soon told her, "You've got to move on." Her employer had to consider replacing her and couldn't wait much longer. All the sympathy and advice she received would go only so far. I jolted her into realizing she had to take charge of herself—or else. That time in her life needed a period, end, conclusion and STOP. Nothing else was acceptable. Many times when I'm engaged for a coaching project, I give people a (verbal) shove. Get over it! I'm the *bearer of bad news*. The fact is that I'm there because company executives care about them and want them to deliver a higher quality of work. Management finds me, hires me and pays for my services. I come in for two full days, and I'm very direct. I'm honest (no sugar coating) and map out what each individual must accomplish. There are no ifs, buts or maybes. Someone has to *tell it like it is*. I know how to present that information to an executive assistant, and because I had worked in the profession for twenty years prior to starting Office Dynamics, they take what I have to say to heart. They know I am not the enemy but a coach and expert in their profession.

On a personal level, my sister, Gina, sometimes does this for me and vice versa. There's a time for a deliberation (when you use the question-mark) and a time to let it go. *Get out of that funk already*! I hasten to add that no one should overlook the seriousness of depression that requires medical intervention. Often times, however, an individual needs only to hear from someone that he or she must put a period on that piece of life and move on. Author, artist, speaker and entrepreneur Vivian Greene tells us, "Life is not about waiting for the storm to pass ... it's about learning to dance in the rain."

Chapter Twelve

The Next Time You Forgive Someone

"Anger makes you smaller, while forgiveness forces you to grow beyond what you were."
—CHERI CARTER-SCOTT

I vividly remember sitting on the floor in my office while being frozen in fear. There had been a break-in while I was out of town working with clients. The thief had violated my space, stolen my belongings and had thrust a stake into my life. After a time, I realized that it's a burden to carry bitterness around and when you can't forgive; bitterness hangs onto you. Still, it was not a small thing to forgive. You already know I believe God has a plan for each of us. Why part of his plan was a robbery of my office, I'll never know. But this I do know … I can't feel *warm and safe* knowing God is with me and has a plan for me only when things are good or slightly puzzling. It's an all-the-time way of life for me, and God wants me to be forgiving. I have also learned that some answers won't be revealed for a long, long time. And by now, I know some answers will never arrive. (As one of my more crusty acquaintances says, "Get over it.")

I've had to forgive people for one thing or another from time to time, and hopefully people have forgiven me for hurts I certainly didn't mean to inflict. But nothing stands out so completely in my psyche as what I share with you now.

Other than me, there was one full time employee working at the Office Dynamics, Ltd. office. The majority of the Office Dynamics team was independent contractors or trainers who lived out of state. I was out of town working with a new, major corporate client. When the employee left the office at lunchtime … we were robbed! She returned to find drawers pulled out, chairs and other things in disarray and all our equipment missing (computers, faxes, and copiers). She called my husband, Dave, right away, and he immediately went to the office. Soon after Dave arrived, she ran out of the office and never returned. I'm enormously thankful that she wasn't there when the robbery took place and I understand she must have been very frightened, but her response added immeasurably to my problem. There was no one to run my office or to assist Dave to keep things running until I returned.

When I got the call from Dave, I had been taking a short nap in my hotel room. I rarely do this, but for some reason I was tired that day. When I answered the phone, Dave told me what happened. I was in shock. I couldn't believe what he was telling me. I had to give a speech the next morning to a large live audience, and we were going to Webcast as well for their virtual assistants. If this had been an endurance test, it couldn't have been better designed! My assistant spoke to me for a few minutes. After the call I thought, "We'll get through this. Dave will be at the office to help until I return." The woman gave notice and left the very next day while I was still in California. I learned of this when I telephoned Dave during a break in my presentation, and I knew I was in a real jam. I was out of town, no one was there to run my office and there wouldn't be an assistant when I returned. On top of everything else, this happened in April, one of the busiest times of the year in my business. Dave couldn't do much since he wasn't familiar with the clients and certainly didn't know where a list of serial numbers for all our equipment could be found. He wasn't working as a company employee or consultant then. He assumed that role much later on.

When I returned to the office, I did not feel safe. I jumped at any little sound. I actually broke down and cried more than once during those early days. One day I was feeling especially anxious, and I called my sister, Gina. "Why don't you go home?" she asked. As far as I was concerned, that wasn't an option. I had a business to run. I was very concerned that client information or financial information had been compromised. (Thankfully it was not.) I really couldn't think of myself, and I worked hard to put my focus elsewhere. I knew that I had to push through the fear rather than succumb to it. I knew if I did not do it that day, I most likely would not do it the next.

When I was out of the office, I felt vulnerable. Was someone watching me? Obviously someone had known when my assistant went out to lunch. That someone had to be watching. My employee took her lunch hour at the same time every day. The thief must have known she drove a red car. Were we—was I still under surveillance? That eerie feeling lingered for many months.

Dave replaced the stolen equipment the next day. The bigger loss was the information contained on the computer hard drives. We did not have our own server because at the time we just weren't that big. Back up files were made on discs, but my employee had neglected to do back-ups for many weeks. She had left recent back-ups in her computer, which, of course, had been stolen. It took six months to build 80 percent of the information back, and then we slowly added pieces of information here and there. The good news was that I always kept hard copies of every seminar, workshop and speech hand-out with my personal notes on them. I kept hard copies of important company information and kept these off-site. I needed to hire someone to input all this information onto the new computers, and it was a time-consuming and therefore costly process.

Did I forgive the perpetrator(s)? You know I did because I had to forgive. I never saw the robbers, and so I didn't have anyone to "hate" for this disruption of my life, business and security. Even though I couldn't put a "face" to the source, I conjured up feelings of forgiveness.

In April 2011, three months after Dave died, my staff and I were in our new and wonderful office for one week, and … I had a déjà vu experience. The ADT security people called me on Sunday to say alarms were blaring at the office. They sent people to the office and did a complete check, and everything was in order. No doors were jammed, no windows were unlocked or broken. One reasonable explanation was the many ceiling sensors that were installed could have been triggered by the extreme winds the area experienced that Sunday.

I realized I could not live my life in fear that a perpetrator would invade our space again. By now, I was fully trained in how to respond. God gave me the strength to get through all of this and through my experience with Dave. I have learned how to put on my shield of courage when facing any situation that can be intimidating. I trust in the Lord.

The next time you are *injured* by others, see if you can find it in your heart to forgive without delay. In order to Live a BIG Life, forgiveness is all in a day's work. You don't have to write a sonnet or dress for the occasion. You have only to say, "I forgive you." And one thing more … you must mean what you say. You can stamp your feet, shout at the top of your lungs, complain to your spouse or a close friend and shed tears but then … forgive, pardon and excuse.

Chapter Thirteen

Superwoman is Missing and It's Okay (a self-examination)

"Superwoman: An extremely accomplished woman, esp. one able to do many things well and often, specif., one equally successful in dealing with the demands of work and family."

See: www.yourdictionary.com/superwoman

When Dave was fighting pancreatic cancer, I hated it when someone would say to me, "We are all going to die someday." Or someone would mention, "So and So's husband had a heart attack and never was the same again. He died last week." I suppose these conversationalists were trying to console me, but their words had the opposite effect.

I would appear to listen politely, but afterwards I studiously avoided these people. They were capable of *sucking the life out of a person,* and although I'm equal to many challenges, I would not rise to this occasion. If I left my superwoman abilities out of this equation, it was okay with me. No one says we have to be perfect. And it's such a relief to know that from time to time superwoman is allowed (and wise) to be missing in action.

On the other hand, when Dave was very sick, some people would ask if they could cook a meal for us or go to the supermarket for me. *No. No. I don't want to impose.* I was walking around with a superwoman attitude, and although I can take care of several things at once and I am strong, I realized I had to let people help me. That was the hard part. Throughout my life, Dave and I had some tough spots, but we always figured out a way to maneuver and we came out on top. With Dave's cancer I realized there was no control and no way out. This was a different kind of cancer, a different beast. We were buying time.

My superwoman persona shimmied in and out of my days. I wanted "her" there, and yet I wanted her gone. *Give me a break!* This dual role got to be exhausting. I put my faith in God. I knew He had a plan and I had to trust in him and hold myself together and keep moving forward. Sometimes I was superwoman and sometimes I was not, and that was that.

I'm with lots of people almost daily. Sometimes I'm with twenty-five women for eight hours a day and sometimes for two or three days in a row. And then I'll meet clients for dinner after I've been presenting all day. When I'm in my office, I may have multiple conference calls scheduled. So when I say I sometimes cherish being alone, you know I am sincere! Since I travel so much, I often eat in restaurants and can't help but notice the other diners. I witness all kinds of curious behaviors, and some recollections still make me shudder. Not only is it okay for superwoman to be missing on occasion … it's a highly recommended condition.

I don't always have the answers to questions and sometimes can't get an answer by asking others or by checking records. Sometimes I have to wait for answers and trust that they will come. This takes patience, and in order to Live a BIG Life it's essential to have patience! Thank goodness we have people to slow us down!

There was some remodeling underway at my house eleven months after Dave passed. When I hired the tile installer, he told me the work could be finished in ten days. I anticipated the work would be completed by that particular date, and I was looking forward to it. But when I spoke to my dad, who has been in the remodeling business for sixty years, he told me to be patient. "This is a big investment. Take your time." The tile contractor told me that we had to take off the shower head and do this and that, and I agreed with his logic, but the finish-date was going to come and go, and that bathroom and shower would still be torn apart. I was scheduled to conduct several workshops and would be far from home, and that was the main reason finishing on time was important to me. Admittedly, I wasn't magnanimous about the situation, but it forced me to slow down and pay attention to the good news; namely, I was going to have a beautiful new bathroom and shower. If I had not been in such a hurry I may have examined more tile colors, textures and designs and chosen differently. I suspect this is so since the people in the show-room sent a tile sample after I had made a selection, and I liked the late arrival very much. Superwoman learned a lesson! That's good news too.

When it has been a number of days since *my superwoman* has made an appearance, I may reach out to buddies or mentors. Mentors are not people I see regularly, and some of my mentors come and go and come again. I had a spiritual mentor for a while, and he still mentors me from time to time. When I first started speaking, Linda Miles mentored me for two consecutive years. Linda is a seasoned speaker, and *I wanted to be her*! Once I was ready for prime time, I didn't need Linda's mentoring. I serve as a mentor for several assistants who want to eventually set up their own training companies. Once they get comfortable they won't need to call upon me, and I'll have time to serve others.

Buddies are different from mentors, and most of us need buddies and mentors. Buddies tend to have a permanent place in our lives.

Each and every day it's possible that you *touch* someone's life. Some of Dave's nurses were phenomenal. They may not know what they meant to us or how I admired them, but I guess knowing you can make a difference in someone else's life helps you to Live a BIG Life.

I relate very well to career-oriented women, and some of my best friends are successful females, but they don't all live nearby. Some are my clients, so I don't get to chat with them all the time. They are busy executives like me, so we don't even get to talk by phone. There's one particular woman in Louisville I absolutely adore. She is a client, and I view her as a mentor. We try once a year to connect by telephone, and if I ever go into Louisville, we dine and talk. When we dine and talk we talk *girl stuff*, too. We'll discuss family, upcoming vacation plans and relatives who disappoint us. I relate to women who are go-getters, who are action oriented and who like to *reach for the stars*. It doesn't mean they don't have struggles. My best friend Ruth is a perfect example. Ruth and her husband run a huge real estate business here in Vegas. Ruth is up at 5:00 AM working out; she attends Boot Camp. She's five years older than I am, and she has boundless energy. She says to me, "Life Is Good, Life Is Good." She'll say this even when I know she is going through a horrible time. Dave used that phrase too. "Life Is Good." My across-the-street neighbor, Sharyn, and I are both widows. She retired from teaching years ago when her husband got sick and she became his caregiver. I mentioned her earlier in this book. She spent fourteen years as his caregiver. She's intelligent and fun to be with, and we support each other. She saved my day not too long ago when my grandson somehow stopped up the commode in the front of the house and there was water gushing all over my new carpet. I called Sharyn, and she knew exactly what to do because she had to do it herself. I am sure most single women would have known what to do, but this had not been my territory for years. When my *superwoman* stepped out, Sharyn's *superwoman* took over! We help each other in a lot of ways. Each of us was married more than thirty years, and we desperately miss our spouses. We did, however, reluctantly share this observation with one another: being alone has some positive sides to it. You don't have to answer to your husband!

I have a great friend in Mary. She is in her early 60s, and she loves to cook and invites me to her house. She lost her husband to cancer too. I'm grateful that Mary knows me well enough to know that when I finish my day's work I often need to go home and do what I call my *internal work*. I'm eager to be peaceful. I write, read or take a walk with the dogs. That's it.

I'm not one to sit around and chit chat, asking, "What's the latest gossip? Did you hear what's going on with Jennifer Anniston or with Angelina Jolie?" Or some people talk about their kids. I don't want to hear about your kids for four hours. I have my own kids and love children, but I don't need to hear all the intricacies for several hours. I like to talk to men a lot because they are interesting and offer different perspectives. I learn a lot. Clearly I have a small group of friends or buddies. I'm blessed to have them, and it comforts me to know I can reach out to any one of them and I'll get a response that won't disappoint.

Chapter Fourteen

Connecting With Others ... Schmoozing

"I define connection as the energy that exists between people when they feel seen, heard, and valued; when they can give and receive without judgment; and when they derive sustenance and strength from the relationship."

—BRENE BROWN

Sometimes all I want to do is talk to a sympathetic someone who will listen. I'm not looking for solutions, but I need to *vent*. When I hear myself explaining a point, I may hear the solution that had escaped me before I *opened up* to another person.

As I go through every day, I build relationships with people and never know where those relationships are going to take me. I'm attentive to building quality relationships. I try to learn about people, what they do for a living, if they have children, any hobbies and what their philosophy of life is to see how we can connect. When conversations begin, I soon learn what we have in common and realize which people fascinate me. After a few conversations, I sometimes say, "No. I don't want to continue with this discourse because this person isn't someone with whom I feel comfortable." I can't, for example, be comfortable with someone who has a tendency to *stretch the truth*. When personal values don't align, I only see wasted time ahead and I don't pursue this relationship. I have no doubt that people come into our lives for a reason. They often "arrive" just when you need them. Sometimes you may be the one arriving just when you're needed! I want to be "that person" as often as possible!

Dave and I met when I was living in Cleveland, Ohio, and working as an Executive Secretary/Receptionist in the corporate offices of Fabric-Centers. (Talk about connecting! Talk about schmoozing!)

The company owned more than three hundred Jo-Ann Fabric Shops, and I reported to a Vice President who oversaw all the District Supervisors and District Managers. My desk was in a beautiful reception area that was surrounded by floor-to-ceiling windows. I was divorced and dating different men, but I wasn't in a serious relationship. One day there was a lot of talk in the office about a twenty-six year old young man who was the youngest Store Manager in the history of Jo-Ann Fabrics and how he had just been promoted to District Manager. *His name was Dave Burge.* Margaret, who was the CEO's Executive Assistant, said to me,

"Who knows, Joan, he might be someone for you to meet?" I thoroughly doubted it! But Dave Burge eventually came into our Cleveland office, and the rest (as they say) is history! The short version of "How Joan & Dave Met" goes like this: Dave and I spoke weekly since all managers had to call me to give me specific store information. Dave was always so nice. He was courteous and drew "smiley faces" on his paperwork. I learned that he too was divorced, and so we each had a great appreciation of what the other had experienced. He lived in Minneapolis and was responsible for business activity in five states. Eventually we started talking to one another at night. I was living with my parents. Dad paid the phone bills. Dave was living on a very tight budget but would call me and we would talk for an hour. We hung up the phones, and I would call him and we talked for another hour. It was so easy to talk to Dave. We discussed all kinds of things: past marriages, what we wanted out of life and world events. Suddenly I was receiving cards in the mail and original poetry that was flowery and flattering. After three months of this long-distance courting, Dave asked me to marry him. "I'll stop smoking if you marry me," he said over the phone one night. Smoking was hardly an issue. The fact is I couldn't even remember precisely what Dave looked like. Did he wear eyeglasses? With only a three month long-distance telephone courtship, one would think we were a couple most likely not to succeed. We married. I moved to Minneapolis although Dave didn't stop smoking for many years. And succeed we did ... thirty-four years of marriage confirms it.

///////

In order to Live a BIG Life, you have to get out of your familiar environment. A writer I know is learning French via an audio course. A 70-something neighbor is taking Zumba (dance) classes. Not only are these individuals learning new things, but they meet people who share their interests. Networks grow; branches shoot off in various directions and attract the attention of others. When you need a plumber, for example, you recall that the Fitness Center owner has a brother who is a plumber. You contact him and expect him to be honest and capable. The personal reference helps to establish that expectation. Are you correct more often than not? I'm not prepared to quantify this assertion, but, empirically speaking, people I engage via *grapevine recommendations* don't disappoint.

I've always been *a ham*. I suspect this aspect of my nature makes it easier for me to be a public speaker and easier to *schmooze* with strangers, many of who in short order become friends. For that I'm grateful. People ask me if I attended Toastmaster meetings to help me prepare for public speaking. No. Speaking in front of groups of people feels natural. When our kids were seven and eight, Dave and I took them to Epcot Center at Disneyworld. We were in the Italian Village, and I volunteered to participate in a small drama in a street scene. I got right into it. I guess it was reminiscent of something I related to when I was young. Put me in front of a room of twenty people and automatically my voice projects. Being Italian I automatically *talk with my hands*. I project even when I'm talking to you. I feel as though I'm speaking loudly, but all that is a part of me now. My instructors, if you can call them that, were all the speakers I admired. I studied everything they did on stage. I modeled what I admired. I incorporated what was natural to me, and before I knew it, my professional speaking persona had a shape and form. I didn't want to be like everyone else, and when I found my style I knew I'd have to be vigilant. I enhance my presentations with ever-changing music, visuals and choreography. People today need to be entertained. They want information, but they also want showmanship. Everyone is accustomed to a quick pace. I'm constantly challenging my listeners to keep them energized, and I am always challenged on ways to enhance my presentation. How do I add the "wow" factor? I learn as much from my audiences and workshop attendees as they do from me. I deliberately stay tuned in so that I learn from them. After all, schmoozing is not a solo pursuit.

Chapter Fifteen

Make Room for Courage

"Your time is limited, so don't waste it living someone else's life.
Don't be trapped by dogma—which is living with the results
of other people's thinking. Don't let the noise of others' opinion
drown out your own inner voice. And most importantly, have the
courage to follow your heart and intuition."
—STEVE JOBS

I could never write a chapter about courage without mentioning Dave and the courage he displayed throughout his ordeal with pancreatic cancer. Dave attended the last Office Dynamics conference in 2010 when he was horribly weak and run down. I realized he wanted to be there for me, and I didn't dissuade him. I believe it was his deep and abiding courage that allowed him to overcome all the reasons why he should have been home in bed and instead was with us at the Red Rock Resort.

When I wanted to start Office Dynamics in 1990, Dave was not a cheerleader. When I shared my vision with him and laid out my dreams, he was quick to trample them. I'm not sure why people—friends, co-workers and loved ones—express doubt when there's something great that we want to do and say things like, "Oh, you better slow down."

Why can't we celebrate each other's dreams and lift up each other and encourage each other instead of saying things like, "You're taking on too much"? As you can tell, eventually Dave did a major turn-around and supported my dream to the hilt, but it took time. As a matter of fact, it took a long time. I had been working as a high level executive assistant for the better part of twenty years. That meant a regular income, paid vacations, medical benefits and a pension plan, and Dave was very comfortable with it all. It meant that I didn't travel, and we had an enviable lifestyle going for us until that day that I came home and told him about wanting to start my company.

Dave didn't do anything to encourage me for one year. He was a nervous wreck. If you knew Dave, you would know he always worried about finances even though we had plenty of money, plenty in terms of being able to take care of ourselves. I had my vision, and he was scared to death. I am a strong person and don't give up easily, and I'm willing to take risks. What did I do for that entire year? I listened to Brian Tracy's motivational tapes. I played them in my car every single day. I read motivational books. I jointed the National Speakers Association and attended meetings. So for one whole year, Dave was not my go-to person, and I actually had to tune him out. I acted as though I had a bubble surrounding me, and when he spoke against what I was doing, I let his words bounce off. I had a passion and was determined to help assistants improve the quality of their work life. The second year, Dave was getting a little better about it. He realized I wasn't going to give up on my dream. And I was actually earning some money, which I hadn't achieved in the first year. And then as he saw that I could do this, he started supporting me fully. And that support got stronger and stronger and eventually he was the one telling me, "Get out of here. What are you doing at home? You should be on the road speaking." He became this huge champion for me. He was guiding me and being my internal consultant, and yet even when he was my champion and I wanted to try something "radical" such as a seminar cruise for assistants you could see the fear and doubts come to life again.

Pay attention to someone who isn't supporting you. No matter how close a person is to you, that person will get in your way if you're not alert. My dad could have sustained a phenomenal business. He had the vision and the talent, but something was lacking. It's difficult for me to be unbiased … this is my dad and I *love him to bits* … but maybe he didn't surround himself with people who believed in him without reserve. When people aren't engaged they often *step on your head.* They don't mean to and may not do it intentionally, but they can hold you down. It's essential to be aware of this phenomenon; those with whom you are closest may hurt you the most. Steve Jobs expresses it well in the quotation above. Have the courage to follow your heart and your intuition.

I understand that God wants you and me to be the best version of ourselves. Still some people disappoint when we have every right to expect the "best" from them. I read something about disappoint-ment, and it resonated with me. "It was one of those times you feel a sense of loss, even though you didn't have something in the first place. I guess that is what disappointment is—a sense of loss for something you never had." (You'll find this observation in "The Nature of Jade" by Deb Caletti.) Still, I almost gag when I think about people who disappoint in this way because I've seen so many courageous people who have lost body parts and eye sight and who have come through all kinds of hardships, and they rise up and act. They don't disappoint! They show courage over and over again.

///////

Some time ago a neighbor invited me to a party. It was the night before New Year's Eve, and Dave had been gone for one year. I decided to dress up and go to the party. I wasn't dressed in a gown, but I was wearing black slacks and a very pretty sweater with a decorated neckline that was flattering. I coordinated my jewelry with great care, and it truly enhanced the outfit. When I arrived at my neighbor's home, I immediately noticed the other guests were dressed in very casual clothing. I needed a little courage to keep from running home and changing my clothes. Admittedly, that required a miniscule grain of courage. Still, as much as it's a small thing, it's also a big thing. I felt good about my appearance and didn't succumb to my initial urge to leave and return in more casual dress. We can be courageous and not be smart. We have to be smart too. If everyone in attendance had been dressed in their "Sunday best" and I had been dressed in pool clothese (my neighbor has a pool) ... I would excuse myself and return in a more appropriate outfit.

Adults frequently discuss teenagers' strong need to be like their peers and do as they do; we sometimes are *guilty as charged*. Go on; get into the habit of mustering courage to follow your heart and intuition!

I love what Mark Twain says about courage. He says courage is mastery of fear, not absence of fear. When I first started speaking, I was frightened. I started Office Dynamics because I wanted to help administrative and executive assistants improve the quality of their work life, rise to higher levels, reduce stress and feel greater satisfaction. Speaking was the vehicle by which I would do this. So when I started speaking, I was afraid, but I had the courage to push through it. I would feel nauseous and light-headed but had courage at the same time. I believe we can feel the fear but courage can outshine the fear. It's up to us to choose. I am not perfect at this. Remember, I am not superwoman. I am better at it than I ever was and hope to get better with each day. I hope it takes me less time to bounce back each time I have a setback. Motivational speaker Les Brown says, "If you have to fall down, I hope you land on your back. If you can look up, you can get up."

Chapter Sixteen

Celebrate Every Birthday Just Like My Dad

"Love life, engage in it, give it all you've got.
Love it with a passion, because life truly does give back,
many times over, what you put into it."
—MAYA ANGELOU

It's notable that you were born and there's no one like you in the world! Yet to a lot of people, a birthday is no big deal. My dad is not one of those people. His birthday is on March 31, the last day of the month, and every March, he starts celebrating on March 1. Some would criticize an entire month of celebration. Well, that's my dad for you. He enjoys himself. I believe that each person has a special gift. You are responsible for recognizing what it is and bringing it forth to the world. My dad doesn't celebrate his birthday to tell the world that he's wonderful. That's not it. What he is saying is, "I'm here and I can contribute. I can make others happy or stronger or safer or something better than if I weren't around to make a difference." His children and grandchildren get more from him in March than birthday cake. They get the message that each one of us is important and each one of us has a job to do.

Dave passed away on January 3, 2011. My children and I were dreading the arrival of January 3, 2012. I had been *down* all year when the holidays and celebration times arrived. A few days before January 3, I chose to make this a wonderful evening of celebration. I made a fine dinner for the eight of us and set the dining room table with beautiful plates. I purchased balloons we could release later in the evening in his honor. We had a celebration of Dave's life. If I had been sitting on the couch in a robe when my family arrived, how would they feel? How would I feel?

The previous four years I was watching Dave after he was diagnosed, and I saw that in one minute his whole life changed. We don't get a second chance. I watched him struggle and wish that he could work. But even to get out of bed each day was a struggle. And then it hit me hard that life really goes fast. When you're young, you're invincible. You can go and leap off a mountain. You don't know that you can get hurt. In our fifties some of us begin to feel that there is fragileness to life, and we know we can't go back. Watching Dave made me realize that every single day I get up is a gift. Please, don't take it for granted. Don't assume that you're going to get up with the sun tomorrow. And when you do get up, enjoy every single part of that day, even the hardships. I'm not saying that every day is easy for me now, even though my business is thriving. I miss Dave. I still get emotional and cry. Then I stop and think that this is my life. It's a gift that I get to wake up today. I get to go out and walk and breathe and take in the sunshine or the clouds and admire the snow on the mountains. Please, don't wait until something traumatic happens to wake up to this reality. Enjoy life now! We either become the victim or the victor. I'm determined not to let anything crush me, especially after I've come this far and worked this hard. I've got a great partner … GOD, of course. I don't want people to think I'm this powerful person. I have the support of friends, of family, my attorney, my doctors and my finance people. I have wonderful grandchildren (Bradley, Madison, Eian and Ethan). I'm not out here doing this by myself but mentally … I am. I need the team around me to help me accomplish what I want to accomplish, and I certainly don't want to do this alone. That wouldn't be any fun.

How clever my dad is to celebrate every day of his birthday month. My dad is a victor too.

I'm reading a book called "The Rhythm of Life" by Matthew Kelly. One of my workshop attendees gave it to me. I can't put the book down. What is in my heart is in his book as well. I notice that all the people who inspire me have had to overcome tragedies. I wonder why that is. Do you know?

Chapter Seventeen

Who Am I Now?

"Knowing others is wisdom,
knowing yourself is enlightenment."
—LAO TZU

I had not been a single woman for a long time. After thirty-four years as a married woman, I was venturing onto new territory. I happened to be a wife who really liked and loved her husband. Dave spent the last six months of his life in our bedroom. He was painfully ill, tormented by this ugly cancer that was ravishing his entire being. The room had become a hospital room. Nurses came to the house three or four times a week for his general checkup, *the vitals.* I was his twenty-four-hour, seven-days-a-week nurse, and I did it with great love and care. That bedroom represented too many endings to a part of my life that I loved. For nine months after Dave died, my nights were filled with restless sleep if I slept at all. It became obvious to me that I had to redecorate the room. Dave was a great shopper and decorator. This was a job for Dave, not for me. I don't like details and get impatient when I have too many options, and I certainly don't like going through catalogs, looking at color swatches and tile samples. Dave would narrow choices down, show me three of the "finalists" and say, "Pick one."

From time to time, I realized I was truly alone in this house. When would this ordeal end? Dave was gone. I had to come to grips with this reality. I took steps to get the bedroom redecorated.

When your youngest child moves out to attend college, you may find yourself living in an "empty nest." The same thing happens after a divorce. You may lose your job or retire and suddenly you wonder, "Who am I? What now?"

Do I know "Joan," really know her, her likes and dislikes? I don't, for example, have to consider whether or not Dave would approve of a flowered fabric to use when upholstering the bedroom chair. After years of *two-heads-planning* I'm not sure if I approve or disapprove. *Who am I?* Little by little I'm introducing me to myself. I'm a successful business woman, confident and assertive, a mother and a grandmother, but I'm not well acquainted with this Joan who is acting alone. I realize I must be patient. William Shakespeare said it this way: "How poor are they who have not patience! What wound did ever heal but by degrees."

Recently someone asked me about my likes and dislikes (e.g., do you read biographies?). I could answer easily since I know *the old me*. I love to learn about people who are successful in business. I recently read a detailed magazine article about Suzy Orman, the internationally known finance expert. I also like to be active! Time spent in the gym or out walking the dogs suits me just fine. Hiking trails and being with my grandchildren playing games are "likes" that beckon to me. On the other hand, one of my favorite pastimes is sitting near the ocean. If I had my choice, I'd sit near the ocean all day. I'd sit and read books (preferably inspirational books). I'd intersperse that with walking along the shore-line. I love the water. I love looking at it and seeing how it changes form. I travel all the time for my work, and since I live in Las Vegas, where some thirty-nine million tourists arrive annually to enjoy their leisure time, I also like to be home to take advantage of the finest restaurants and entertainment. I live in a beautiful guard-gated community that's built up against the mountains. It's very easy to be in this beautiful place! When I travel for pleasure, I like to travel with my children and grand-children. I suspect when the children reach their teen years they won't want to travel with Grandma, and I will figure out what to do at that time. The first year Dave passed away, I rented a house on Torch Lake in Michigan. This actually was Dave's idea the previous year when he was on his "I'm going camping" marathon. I read somewhere that The National Geographic Society named Torch Lake the *Third Most Beau-tiful Lake in the World*. In May 2012, we went to Disneyworld for nine days. That was a wild trip. A trip to Italy is on my two-years-from-now agenda. I anticipate taking my Lauren and Brian with me since that is where their great-grandparents were born.

Something else I LIKE is learning! I have always been a sponge soaking up anything I could from any good person. But I also observed what behaviors I didn't like in people and what didn't work well in the business world. I want to learn everything I can because I'm storing it. It will be there for me to access in the future. I try to make connections. I read and hear and ask, "Can I connect this to anything I'm doing? Can I pass it along to someone who I know may need it?" Apparently I'm still the same *connector* I was when Dave was alive. I still carry my invisible bag. I take it with me wherever I go. So naturally I had it with me this week on my consulting project. I was taking in, absorbing what I learned from the people I was there to help. I was observing the executives. I was working in a department in an industry that was totally new to me. All the bits and pieces of know-how I acquired were placed inside my invisible bag. A woman who lives a BIG Life automatically cultivates her knowledge base. Sometimes at the end of a day, I (figuratively speaking) dump the contents of that bag onto the floor. I look over my acquisitions and then return them to the bag.

All of the time-tested skills I introduce to others are there for me to use too. If I catch myself in what I call a low mood, I know I've got to flip it over. I ask, "What are the lessons I can learn from this situation?" I have to change my thinking … lighten up and be positive. I know that if I get too absorbed in negative thinking, I've got to *get the heck out of there*. It's a bad place to be. I'm still the Joan who knows better.

As to the rest of *Who Am I Now*: I'll just have to stick around and find out.

Afterword

Afterword

This part of a book is reserved for a short essay, usually written by the author. I was inspired to write this essay before I wrote this book. *A Hummingbird made me do it!* In February after Dave passed away, I was sitting outside on my patio early in the morning trying to think of ideas for my next Office Dynamics administrative conference when the humming bird appeared. Dave loved hummingbirds and would try to attract them to our yard with feeders placed everywhere.

A few months later, as I was carrying groceries from my car that was parked in the driveway, a large hummingbird flew into my garage and fluttered around the ceiling for about five minutes. I believe this bird was letting me know that Dave's soul had made the final journey. The beautiful bird was a good omen. I felt sure Dave was at peace and he was my champion in Heaven.

Then again, on October 15, 2011, (the first anniversary of Dave's birthday since he passed) another little hummingbird was fluttering around a window under the patio roof. I just happened to be standing in the living room at that very moment. It was as though the bird wanted to get my attention. I looked out and said, "Happy Birthday Dave!"

We Had A Good Ride

Throughout our thirty-four year marriage, Dave and I had a lot of rocky times, but we had many more good times. As we have all heard, a good long-lasting marriage takes work—and it does!

About one year after Dave had been diagnosed with pancreatic cancer and finished seven months of bi-weekly intense treatments, went through three major surgeries and was on the mend, he actually was enjoying some of the things in life he had forgotten how to enjoy. He was able to be a wonderful consultant for Office Dynamics with a flexible schedule that fit his follow-up chemo and radiation treatments; he was able to enjoy a lovely dinner like we used to do; he finally even got to play a few rounds of golf. It was at this time we had "the discussion." Not the one about him dying as he never talked about that—he always said and even wore a hat that said "Life is Good." The discussion was about, "Well, we had a good ride, didn't we?"

And we did! I am thankful to God for the many blessings he poured on us throughout our thirty-four years. We had two beautiful children, Lauren and Brian, and Dave had a wonderful son, David Wade. We got to do the *fun things* you do with children, and we specially loved camping with them when we lived in the Carolinas, Virginia and Michigan. We sat around many crackling fires for hours roasting marshmallows and listening to the lapping water. We went on fabulous vacations including Disneyworld and a magnificent cruise when the kids became young adults. We really laughed a lot on that vacation. It was pretty wild, actually. Dave and I went on eight cruises, all full of adventure, love, fun, meeting new people, dancing, laughing, hugging and kissing! In fact, when I turned thirty, Dave surprised me with my first cruise. He was always surprising me whether it was fresh flowers or a table set with beautiful new dishes or a new outfit—he poured his love on me in many ways beyond physical affection. We were friends before we became husband and wife.

Thanks to all of Dave's promotions and fantastic career, we traveled to beautiful, tranquil, tucked-away resorts with casitas or traveled to London. We had beautiful homes although our first home was twenty-six years old and we laughed our way through trying to remodel it ourselves because we didn't have money to hire a professional contractor. We skied, played racquetball, golfed, went swimming often, water-skied, cooked out, camped, danced until all hours of the night, enjoyed many quaint dinners with good friends and laughed and laughed and danced and danced. Life was good, and we had a good run. I know it was not in God's plan for Dave to continue this journey with me. And as hard as that is for me to accept only being a widow for a short time, I understand God had a different plan for Dave and he has a plan for me. Dave Burge (born October 15, 1950) lived a BIG Life. He did everything he wanted to do and then some.

Photos

Joan & Cody

Dave & Joan - the younger years

Joan's mom

Joan's mom & dad:
Sandy & Tony

Lauren,
Joan's Dad,
Kelly

Joan's Office Dynamics Angels:
Jasmine & Michele

Burge Family:
Dave, Barb, Pete,
Bob & their mom, Joan

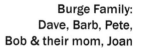

Lauren & Jeff

Brian, Ethan, Eian

Liz, Tony, Joan, Dave

Joan's mother-in-law, Joan

David Wade

Dave's California Angel, Gina

Cody & Joan High Five

Ethan, Eian, Madison, Bradley

Charday, Joan, Tessa

Disney 2012
(from left)
Ethan, Bradley,
Madison, Eian, Joan

Joan's mom

Joan & Dave
Dave's 58th surprise
birthday party

Joan,
Janet,
Gina

Gratitude Journal

Joan's Gratitude Journal Notes

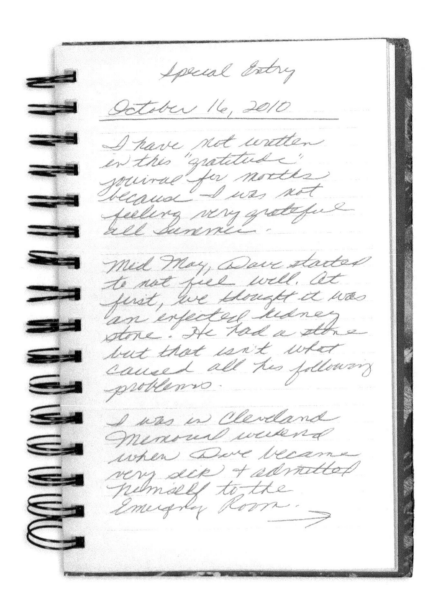

Special Entry

October 16, 2010

I have not written in this "gratitude" journal for months because I was not feeling very grateful all summer.

Mid May, Dave started to not feel well. At first, we thought it was an expected kidney stone. He had a stone but that isn't what caused all his following problems.

I was in Cleveland Memorial weekend when Dave became very sick & admitted himself to the Emergency Room. →

It turned out his
sugar was over 600
& so was his CA19.
Dave was in + out of
the hospital 3 times
in June. Each time
he was admitted, he
was in the hospital
for days.
   We missed our
long planned, big
cruise in June.
   Dave was sick the
entire summer and
still not ~~even~~ too well.
It appears cancer cells
went into his small
bile ducts in the
liver. He has 3
different tubes pro-
truding out of his
body and back on
chemo.
                    ⟶

Rather go on about
our HORRIBLE summer,
I want to say that
I am thankful once
again, God has brought
us thru another scary
time with Dave. We all
thought we were going
to lose him in June.)
Yesterday was Dave's
~~60th~~ ~~birthday and it~~
~~was 3 years since he~~
~~had his first chemo~~
treatment w/ Dr. Isacoff.
I am grateful he is
here, even though he
isn't working or feeling
well.
All our grandchildren
are healthy & well.
I am thankful for
David Wade who
came out here in
June & September ➔

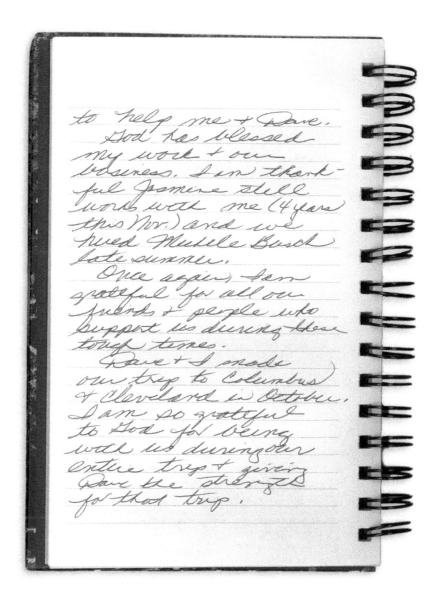

to help me + Dave.
God has blessed
my work + our
business. I am thank-
ful Jasmine still
works with me (4 years
this Nov.) and we
hired Michele Busch
late summer.
    Once again, I am
grateful for all our
friends + people who
support us during these
tough times.
    Dave + I made
our trip to Columbus
+ Cleveland in October.
I am so grateful
to God for being
with us during our
entire trip + giving
Dave the strength
for that trip.

Special Entries

Dave's First Blog

Dave's First Blog

11/17/07 11:56 AM Filed in: <u>Dave writes</u>
Hello to Family and Friends

I just got back from UCLA Medical Center Tuesday night (November12). For some strange reason I thought it would be a piece of cake driving there by myself. It wasn't. (It must be a guy thing) or I just don't want to give in yet and try to continue to do all the things I could do before. I am beginning to realize I can't.

I came home to quite a surprise, but first a little background. Once I was told I had cancer, I told Joan that I really wanted to do up the holidays as much as we could. So Joan did a wonderful job making our home look Halloween with lights and pumpkins everywhere. I had fun handing out the candies and seeing the kids check out her decorations.

But the big surprise was that she told our daughter Lauren what my wish was and Lauren who works for a very large convention exhibit design company named, Czarnowski, mentioned it to her boss, Sam, who is the General Manager. He said that he would take care of everything. He sent out his top designer named, Angelic, to meet with Joan and to see what Christmas decorations we had. This was kept a secret from me. You could never imagine what I came home to Tuesday night. They turned our house into a WINTER WONDERLAND! I think they put in 7 Christmas trees. There is one decorated just for the grandkids, and one for our Lauren and Brian (with ornaments they made when they were little), one in our bedroom, one in the guest bedroom and the rest throughout the house.

Wreaths are everywhere, all our tables and countertops were done up with great care and lots of festivity. Angelic was able to decorate using some of our favorite holiday pieces that we've gotten over the years – David Winter cottages, Joan's Christmas carousel, and several Santas. She graced our family room fireplace with all the stockings for our golden retrievers, grandchildren, and children and she carefully selected the stocking holds for them. Angelic event went out and got all the different holiday candies I like. When I walked in, tears came rolling down my cheeks. Words just cannot explain how I felt. It is always special when someone does something special for you!

It's rather amazing how God works. Who knew 5 years ago when Lauren was hired by Czarnowski that it would lead to this wonderful Christmas present that all our family here and friends will enjoy.

My son, David Wade, came in from Michigan for a week and helped with a lot of things around the house. He hung our Christmas lights on the outside of the house and on trees. He and I got to spend some time alone. It was great to see him.

I cannot even fathom going through this alone. Joan has been at my side from day one and refuses to slow down. I don't know how she does it all – wife, mother, grandmother, business owner and travels to boot. I have got to get her to slow down. The outpouring of family, friends, coworkers, and my bosses is overwhelming. I can't thank you all enough for your thoughts and prayers, cards and letters.

I know many of you have your own issues going on and my thoughts are prayers are with you all. Thank you for taking time to think about me.

Special hugs and kisses to Gina for all she has done for Joan and me. She checks on me everyday and especially when I'm in California. She created this blog and oversees it. She is a winner!

Love and Happy Thanksgiving to all

Dave

Celebration of Life Eulogy—Life is Good
(by Joan Burge)

DAVID ALAN BURGE - 1950 - 2011

LIFE IS GOOD

This is a strange philosophy for man who was battling pancreatic cancer for more than three and one-half years.

David Alan Burge's life ... was good! In fact, he lived a rich, full life and had no regrets. Dave did everything he wanted to do.

So how did I meet this wonderful man? We both worked for the same company—me as a secretary at the big corporate office in Cleveland, OH., Dave as the youngest District Supervisor in the history of Jo-Ann Fabrics—except he lived in Minnesota. Dave reported to my boss, so we talked on the phone all the time and he used to come into the corporate office for management meetings. He was the company rebel who almost got fired because he changed all the fabrics and design of his stores in Minnesota to accommodate a Midwest client. But instead of getting fired, he created a change that rippled through 300 stores nationwide. He loved his job and was liked by all.

Out of all the District Supervisors who reported to my boss, Dave was the only who used to draw smiley faces on his travel itineraries that came to me or would write me a thank you note for assisting with his travel arrangements. Because of his kindness, I sent Dave a card one day just to say thank you for being a nice guy. To this day, Dave would tell you that I was inviting him to call me—but he read more into the lines than what I intended. Before we knew it, we were talking to each other on the phone two hours a night.

After three months of a long-distance-call relationship (and expensive bills), I agreed to marry Dave—even though I couldn't remember that he wore glasses. I moved to Minnesota, and three months later we moved to Cleveland, OH. Being that I never lived away from home, I was homesick; Dave was often on the road, and my dad was very persuasive.

Dave worked in my dad's home remodeling business for eight years. This was no easy feat as this was an Italian-owned family business. Dave was a good student and as always committed to doing his best at whatever he did.

While Dave did not attain the career he thought in my dad's business, he had a much greater blessing—my dad, Anthony DeGirolamo—who taught Dave to embrace the finer things in life. Dave went from being a JC Penny guy with a scrawny red mustache to a sophisticated man with manicured nails. He grew to appreciate the finer things while still being the down-to-earth guy I fell in love with.

During our time in Cleveland, we had two beautiful children: Lauren and Brian. Dave was ecstatic when they came into our life. He loved playing with them and being their dad.

I was blessed to meet Dave's first son, David Wade, who lived in Grand Rapids, Michigan, with his mom. David came to spend time with us every summer. Who knew our love and relationship would blossom into one that I now consider him ... a son.

We did it all, from camping to skiing, playing racquetball, watching Sunday football games, fancy dinners, snowball fights, and being with friends and family.

There were many difficult times, too, as my mother suffered with severe manic depression for many years.

(but) LIFE WAS GOOD.

////////

After eight years, we agreed to pack our belongings, dog and two children and begin our own Dave & Joan Burge life heading south. We didn't have jobs and didn't know what we were going to do and where our home would eventually be. But we were both adventurous, in love and confident we would find our way. We drove off to Greenville, South Carolina, (on my dad's birthday—which he would never let us forget) to live with Dave's parents for a short time.

Eventually Dave accepted a wonderful job as an Account Executive with Naegele Outdoor Advertising in Asheville, North Carolina. This opened an entirely new world for us.

Once again, Dave's spirit to *buck the system* created a big stir with upper management. But eventually he taught them about the finer things in business, which led him to a senior management position in a very short time. He received award after award, letters of recognition, promotions and was so proud of his achievements. Dave was in his glory and loved outdoor advertising.

While living in North Carolina, we often took the kids camping and even went white water rafting. Dave loved living at the base of the Great Smokey Mountains. He enjoyed being with the kids, watching them ride their bikes and attending Lauren's soccer games. Dave also cherished and spent hours working in our yard. He enjoyed watching football and going on cruises—we went on eight!

Dave stayed in the outdoor industry for more than fifteen years. He was highly respected by everyone in the industry, and his employees adored him. Dave was tough and always wanted his employees to be their best—but he was nurturing and kind. During those fifteen years, he went from working for Naegele to Adams Outdoor Advertising, where he fully blossomed beyond imagination. Once again, he was the rebel and he went from overseeing one market to three markets.

We lived in North Carolina, Tennessee, Virginia, and finally … Lansing, Michigan. During those years, David Wade would jump in and out of living with us.

When Dave's career in Outdoor Advertising ended, we stayed in Lansing until the kids finished high school (which wasn't very long after). That is when he stepped into my two-year-old training business and started teaching me to think like a business person vs. a "mom" operation—it has finally sunk in after twenty years!

In Michigan, Dave was active with our children. We would go up to Boyne to ski, go camping, watch Brian ride his skateboard, have snowball fights and walk our two golden retrievers (Annie and Zoe) in the woods across the street from our house.

Lansing is where Dave got heavily involved in the LPGA. He played golf with a young girl, Anika Sorenstam—a nobody at the time—but now the world's greatest female golfer! He followed her entire career, and for his special 58th birthday party, she sent him one of her gloves and autographed golf balls.

///////

In October of 2000, we moved to Las Vegas to experience another part of the United States and start another adventure. For the first time in our marriage, this was my doing. While Dave was retired at the time, he got antsy as he was always a career-man. He was prodded by John and Ruth Ahlbrand (the wonderful people who sold us our home) to get into real estate and work in their company, RE/MAX Central. Dave buckled down and went to real estate school, studied hard and got his license. After a few years as an agent selling, John and Ruth asked Dave if he wanted to manage a second office. Dave immediately said yes. His real strength and heart has always been in management. Through this, the four of us became best friends.

Lauren and Brian blessed him with three beautiful grandchildren who would light up his life and make him smile. His most favorite thing to do with the little ones was swimming and pulling them around on a big turtle raft. Through Brian, Ethan came into our family and has always been dearly loved.

///////

DAVE BURGE LOVED LIFE ...

He loved to played golf with his good friend John at Red Rock Country Club where they constantly razzed each other.

Dave loved going to Rancho Valencia in California to chill out with our good friends John and Ruth.

Dave liked to play craps—especially when my Dad came to visit, and he will never forget the time he met my stepmom, Liz.

He loved fine wine, our golden retrievers and Jack Daniels! We often gathered with friends at our various houses.

LIFE WAS GOOD.

////////

Considering we were the couple most likely to not succeed (knowing each other only three months), we shared thirty-four wonderful, adventurous years of marriage. I learned as much from Dave as he learned from me. Our backgrounds were completely opposite—me a fiery Italian and Dave a strong-minded Irish German. But we blended them to create our own life, and we each embraced each other's family.

Dave was much more than "just a husband." He was my partner, my best friend, my sweetheart and my sounding board.

Dave was my personal shopper—making me try on styles I would never wear—but that always looked great on me once I put the clothes on.

He constantly challenged me to think like a business owner. He was my internal consultant. This was amazing because when he married me, he thought I would always be this little Italian girl who would work as a secretary and cook pasta for him. In time, Dave became my biggest supporter and I will miss him terribly.

Dave Burge was funny, smart, a hard worker and a good friend. He was always interested in the latest and greatest technology tools whether it was a computer or cell phone.

His work ethics were impeccable.

Dave was always proud to be a Burge and of his family.

He had an amazing sense of humor, always with a quick comeback.

Dave always looked like he just stepped out of GQ magazine even when he was getting chemo treatment or heading to a hospital. He used to say, "It is better to look marvelous, than feel marvelous!"

He loved our country and was terribly disappointed when he was young and could not serve with his good friend, Jim, because of a hearing problem.

///////

In September of 2007, after five months of not feeling well, Dave was diagnosed with pancreatic cancer, one of the deadliest and most aggressive forms of cancer with only a 4 percent, five year survivor rate. His battle was long and very hard. It is a story in itself, and I'm certain I will write about his journey some day.

Over the past four years I saw an amazing strength in Dave that I had never seen before. He was a warrior and my hero.

While Dave and his kids were often at odds with many aspects of life, his kids were there when he needed them the most. All three showed up in their own special way, giving Dave the greatest gift of life—unselfish love. Dave was always proud of Wade, Lauren and Brian.

His spiritual life blossomed especially over the past four years. I have personally witnessed the hand of God at work in our lives the past four years, but especially the last seven days of Dave's life. I know Dave is at eternal peace with his Heavenly Father.

As Dave would say ... LIFE IS GOOD.

And Now, The Warrior Returns Home
1995 – by Nancy Fraze

Not the end, but the beginning,
The man speeds his pace,
Cresting over the last hill.

Tho' long, the mission was successful
A smile slips across his face
As he gazes across open meadows.
Morning sun touches his brow
And he hurries onward.

The warrior, weapon in hand.

Fighting fiercely in many battles
Overtaking enemy ground
Facing off in all types of combat.
He's **won**.
His weapon, oft used,
Sharp and sure,
Freed many hurting souls,
Brought health and liberty.

At last, at last!
He sees HOME, and he hurries on,
Then sprints to a run.

The doors of HOME open,
Warm hands and open hearts greet him.
The warrior slips off his dusty robe and sandals,
And replaces them with
Fresh Clean Garments.

With unabashed joy, and anticipation
Grown in battle and decisive triumph,
The warrior approaches his Commander.

Gently drawing his sword, one last time,
He lays it in the hands of his great King.

The King gazes proudly at His warrior,
Who completed a great task, the assignment of Life,
Smiles, grasps his hand and welcomes him:
"Well done, VERY well done, thou good, and faithful servant.
Let all my people and creations celebrate this great warrior's return!
For he has won many battles, fought bravely for My Name,
Successfully overcoming My enemies
At last, at last! My warrior returns Home!"

Not the end, but only the beginning ...

Dave's California Angel, Gina, Writes ...

(May 30, 2012)

For the first 30 yrs. that Dave was my brother–in–law I would say our relationship was typical for siblings through marriage. We would laugh about some things, have a few common interests, respect each other's space and consider ourselves family. The time that Dave & Joan lived in Cleveland their house was like a second home to me and Dave never minded how much time I was there. By the time they left Cleveland I was already off to college and beginning my life as a young adult. We would then see each other on some holidays and vacations and occasionally just say Merry Christmas or Happy Birthday over the phone.

After Joan & Dave moved to Las Vegas in 2001 we began to see each other more often. Even though Dave was very helpful and would always give me some bits of life advice if I was feeling down or despondent, we had very different views on the world. I tried my hand at political debate with him and we very quickly found out that we were complete opposites. Needless to say we would butt heads. So we just began to dance around those kinds of conversations and kept it light, which was ok but didn't really make for full friendship.

When Dave began to feel ill in 2007 he was sent to Cedars Sinai Hospital in Los Angeles for some tests that could not be done in Nevada. Of course since I lived in LA I wanted to escort Dave & Joan on this very important appointment. I just wanted to help out my sis and brother-in-law in any way I could since they were always there for me when I was younger and even as an adult. Once we realized Dave would have to be making multiple trips to UCLA for chemo treatments I offered to pick him up at Burbank Airport and drive him to Dr. Isacoff's office at UCLA which was not always an easy feat in LA traffic. Sometimes Joan would be with him but many times she wasn't because she had to keep her business going. This allowed lots of alone time for Dave and I.

I remember being a little nervous the first time I was to pick him up at the airport. I was thinking, "What will we talk about for so long in the car?" Well I was quite surprised that Dave really opened up to me and just shared with me his feelings and thoughts about what was going to happen. I began to relax and just converse and before you know it we were at UCLA. That night after some dinner I went back to his hotel room to keep him company and we talked for two more hours. I learned that night how to have a conversation with someone with an opposing view and just listen. I wasn't invested in convincing him and he wasn't invested in convincing me. I think we both appreciated that time very much.

Mother Theresa said, "People are unreasonable, illogical and self-centered. Love them anyway." I think this is what Dave and I thought about each other. Sometime during the Vegas to LA trips Joan & Dave started calling me Dave's California Angel. And at the incredible surprise 58th birthday party that Joan threw him they gave me a t-shirt with that on it. I tried to wear that shirt when I would pick him up or visit him in Vegas. As he felt better through 2008 we worked together at Joan's company Office Dynamics and expanded our relationship even further. We really embraced each other and accepted each other.

I saw Dave go through so much during his treatments and surgeries and although much of it was painful he never once complained. To quote Martin Luther King "The ultimate measure of man is not where he stands in times of comfort and convenience but where he stands at times of challenge and controversy." In my eyes, Dave measures up to a courageous warrior always going forward with grace and dignity. I am truly blessed to have been on the journey with Dave from the beginning, to caressing his head in his final breath. I learned how to be big, to embrace my fears of death by being witness to his. I learned to be big, by opening my heart to help him out. I learned to be big, by listening to someone else instead of defending my own thoughts. I learned how to be big, by loving.

Gina

Introducing a Unique Women's Group
20 YEARS & COUNTING

In 1991 Joan Burge approached me about starting a professional women's group. My first thought was … do we really need another organization and do I have the time to add something else to my overflowing to do list? As many of you know Joan is persistent. So the evening I left the podium after presiding over my last meeting as president of the local chapter of Professional Secretaries International, she asked me again. We started brainstorming as to what we liked and disliked about other professional groups. The likes included networking, forming friendships, and learning new things. The dislikes included long and boring business meetings, taking minutes, and fundraising. So we decided to focus on what we enjoyed the most and Star Achievers™ was founded!

Our initial mission statement was "To create a unique and dynamic Association uniting dedicated, high-level administrative professionals for the purposes of professional development, sharing knowledge and business experiences, displaying individual talents, and networking with individuals equal in career status." I believe we have accomplished every goal!

So we began getting together monthly with each member taking a turn hosting a meeting and serving as team leader on an annual basis. I must admit that I never expected us to be together for 20 years! Think about it … how many organizations have you committed to for 20 years? That calculates to approximately 240 meetings! It is hard to believe that we still can find informative and creative topics. We have learned about new technology, car repairs, and health issues, traveled and sailed aboard yachts, bottled wine, visited museums and TV stations, had our handwriting analyzed and our fortunes told, taken cooking, flower arranging and dancing lessons, just to mention a few.

We have shared good times as well as bad times, supported each other during sad and troubled times, and celebrated marriages, children, grandchildren, and promotions. We have laughed until our tummies hurt—the best stress reliever ever.

Although Joan left the area, we never lost touch of our personal relationship. We may not speak for months, but when we get together it seems as there was never any lapse in time. Our conversations are seamless and we always know that we are there for each other if the need ever arises.

Looking back over the past 20 years I do not think that neither Joan nor I ever imagined how special our group would become to each one of us. I only know that I look forward to the next 20 years as our friendship continues to grow and blossom.

Teresa C. Peters
President
Stanton Partners, Inc.
October 2011

Resilience

Resilience is the ability to bounce back, pick yourself up and go on.
It is the power to self-heal, renew and to
always be taking the next step forward.
It is in reconnecting to the line of your life and endeavor,
joining it where it has moved to now, not where you left it last.

Resilience has the quality of robustness;
It is the capacity for spontaneous recover.
The repair, replenishment and recharge
are generated by the will to live and to go on,
and by the determination to take the next step, to proceed forward.
It is the regeneration of all that can be.

You have seen yourself coming to the end of your rope, the end of your
strength,
Reaching a point of despair; to then find a new start and discover a
new day,
To move forward again in a new way and with a new power—that's
resilience.

Resilience knows no end. It has no limits and no boundaries.
It is the fountain of life and living;
The absolution that spring brings to winter;
the unstoppable vine of growth, of love, of beauty and of purpose.
It is the hope passed on from one generation to the next,
and the covenant that there shall always be a new day,
and that you, too, can always make a new start.

LET US RESILIENT ON.

Aviv Shahar

This chapter of my life is closed. But I am not sad;
I am excited to see what God has planned
for my future.

Photo by Brian Burge

Disneyworld 2012 (Coronado Springs Hotel)

You Can't Press Instant Replay
by Joan Burge

You Can't Press Instant Replay
by Joan Burge

Life is long; life is short. Life is sweet; life is bitter. Life is dirt in your face; life is sunshine in your face. Life is a roller coaster; life is a train ride. Life is the smell of freshly cut grass, jasmine flowers in full bloom and freshly baked bread. Life tastes like a mouthful of sourball candy; life tastes like a creamy sweet chocolate.

We cannot hit an **Instant Replay** button. We go around one time, so make it the best. Feel the pain and be exuberant when life is going well.

Don't take people for granted; they may not be here tomorrow. You may not be here tomorrow!

Take East Coast Swing or Hip Hop dance lessons.

Treat a mentor to lunch. It will be one of your best investments.

Roll in the grass on a cool summer evening.

Lie on the grass with your friend and look up at the stars for hours.

GO TO DISNEYWORLD AT LEAST ONCE IN YOUR LIFE, EVEN IF YOU DON'T HAVE KIDS.

Always be honest and ethical. You'll never have to look over your shoulder.

Stroll at a farmers' market and taste all the free samples.

Treat yourself to fresh flowers just because you love yourself.

Own a pet at least once in your life.

THROW YOURSELF A BIG PARTY.

WATCH MANY SUNSETS AND SUNRISES.

Smell jasmine shrubs.

Dig your feet in the sand by the beach and then build sand castles.

DO SOMETHING THAT SCARES YOU.

Tell the important people in your life you love them at least once a week.

Bring flowers to the nurses at your local hospital (just because they care and work hard).

MAGNIFY THE GOOD THINGS IN YOUR LIFE.

Take your dream vacation at least once in life.

Forgive someone who hurt you and against whom you have been holding a grudge for a long time.

Turn up the music loud at home, by yourself, and dance like crazy!

Be the change you want to see in the world.

RIDE AN OLD-FASHIONED BICYCLE.

Always reach for the stars!

Watch Lucille Ball or the Little Rascals with a friend and laugh until you cry.

Do somersaults on the fresh green grass.

Surprise a stranger by doing a good deed.

SURPRISE YOUR NEIGHBORS AND LINE THE STREET WITH LITTLE RED, WHITE, AND BLUE FLAGS FOR WHEN THEY AWAKE 4TH OF JULY MORNING.

FAIL AT SOMETHING. IT WILL BE YOUR GREATEST LESSON.

Eat more ice cream.

Set your table as if you were having company for dinner … it will inspire you to invite friends over for food and good conversation.

WALK FOR MILES ON THE BEACH BY THE OCEAN AND LISTEN TO THE MOTION OF THE OCEAN. SEE THE SPARKLES FROM THE SUN BOUNCE OFF THE WAVES.

Lie still with your hands on your chest, softly breathe and remember that your body is a fine-tuned machine. Appreciate your muscles, heart, bones, skin … this is your vehicle to maintain all your life.

Start singing out loud in a public area.

RIDE IN A STRETCH LIMO AT LEAST ONCE, WITH OR WITHOUT FRIENDS.

Make sure you celebrate your 50th birthday big time!

Be thankful for your hair, even if you only have a little. It may not be there if you get sick or when you get old.

Brush and floss your teeth at least twice a day.

Let the little children in your life know you love them and they are the best gift to the world!

ALWAYS LIFT OTHERS UP, NOT TEAR THEM DOWN. EACH PERSON IS A CHILD OF GOD.

Give big hugs to friends and family you love when you see them the next time.

Save $2 every day for the rest of your life. That's $730/year; in 30 years you will have an extra $21,900 plus interest. Either donate it or splurge on something for yourself or your family.

There are no guarantees in life; enjoy this day and live it as if it were your last day on earth.

Smile! Laugh! Cry! Scream in the mirror! Laugh, again.

LOVE and accept yourself. Let your inner light shine and you will light up the world.

Affirmations and Joanisms

AFFIRMATIONS to Live a BIG Life

I am FEARLESS

I am VIGILANT

I am STRONG

I am SMART

I am CAPABLE

I am CREATIVE

I am TALENTED

I am VICTORIOUS

I am CONFIDENT

I am ANOINTED

I am BEAUTIFUL

I am DETERMINED

I am ENERGY

I am RESILIENT

I am HEALTHY

I am HOPEFUL

I am HAPPY

I am PATIENT

I am COLORFUL

I am THANKFUL

I am ADVENTUROUS

I am GRATEFUL

I am FLEXIBLE

I am COMMITTED

I am BOLD

I am ADAPTABLE

I am COURAGEOUS

I am SKILLED

I am FORGIVING

I am ME!

Joanisms: BIG Thoughts for a BIG Life

*The only way to Live a BIG Life is by filling
your heart with BIG thoughts.
Here are some of my favorite "Joanisms" that I hope you enjoy, too.*

Small thinking leads to a small life. Think BIG.

God is BIG enough to handle whatever I am going through.

God will give me the strength to do what I thought was not possible.

Look at life with a question mark, not a period. (Period means the end; that there is no better way or no answer. A question mark opens the mind to answers and opportunities.)

You cannot see "it," but you step out anyway.

Living a BIG Life is about quality, not quantity or length of time.

Who you are today is not all you are capable of becoming.

I am full of CAN-DO Power!

It takes courage to Live a BIG Life.

It takes courage to let your inner light shine and not follow the crowd.

Pull back from abyss and focus.

Create *Human Moments*™.

Don't feed the 'dragons.'

You are responsible for you. Create your own energy.

Don't set a plate for worry at your table.

Ignite your passion.

Security lies within you, not a job.

You are on stage every day.

I <u>can</u> do this for one more day.

Be willing to lose in order to win.

Life is filled with clouds and bright sunshine. Embrace it all!

There is no instant replay in the game of life.

Stare your fears in the face.

Don't focus on how far you have to go. Focus on the next step.

Let your inner light shine.

No one can intimidate you unless you let them.

Obstacles and barriers are just a test of how badly you want something.

GET OVER IT!

RED LIPSTICK ON!

Joan's Spiritual Messages

Joan's Favorite Spiritual Messages

- Faith is focusing on vision, not obstacles.

- God is more interested in changing you than changing your circumstances.

- Follow the vision of what God wants you to do.

- God is never in a hurry, but he is always on time.

- While we worry about how fast we grow, God is concerned about how strong we grow.

- I will not go through tough stuff alone.

- God doesn't bless mediocrity—he blesses excellence.

- When you stand strong and have a good attitude … pay day is coming your way.

- God has given me the grace for the season I am in.

- Trust in the Lord with all your heart and lean not on your own understanding. (Proverbs 3:5)

- Faith is daring to be a chance-taker.

Joan's Daily Prayer:

Dear God, in Your hands

I place myself on this day.

Your purpose for my life,

Your perfection for my body,

Your abundance to fill my need—

In Your hands lie these,

And their fulfillment in my life

Is sure if by my will and my desire

I, too, am totally in Your hands.

Guide me, then, in Your ways

Throughout the whole of this day—

Free my mind of fear and doubt

That I may think creatively,

Free my body of its limitations

That it may be strong and vital,

Free my spoken word of hesitation

And my action from indecision.

In Your hands I place my total self

For I am Yours, dear Father-God.

(Source: Unity School of Christianity, Unity Village, MO)

Quotes

Live a BIG Life™ Book Chapter Quotes

"In three words I can sum up everything I've learned about life. It goes on."
—*Robert Frost*

"When I stand before God at the end of my life, I would hope that I would not have a single bit of talent left, and could say, I used everything you gave to me."
—*Erma Bombeck*

"Action will lead you forward to the success you deserve."
—*George Clason, author of The Richest Man in Babylon*

"Be ever engaged, so that whenever the devil calls he may find you occupied."
—*St. Jerome*

"A man is a success if he gets up in the morning and gets to bed at night, and in between he does what he wants to do."
—*Bob Dylan*

"The shorter way to do many things is to do one thing at a time."
—*Mozart*

"A man who misses his opportunity, and a monkey who misses his branch, cannot be saved."
—*Hindu Proverb*

"The more you recognize and express gratitude for the things you have, the more things you will have to express gratitude for."
—*Zig Ziglar*

"A well-dressed woman, even though her purse is painfully empty, can conquer the world."
—*Louise Brooks*

"Faith is like the radar that sees through the fog."
                                        —*Corrie Ten Boom 1892 -1983*

"An optimist may see a light where there is none, but why must a pessimist always run to blow it out?"
                                        —*Rene Descartes 1831 - 1901*

"Anger makes you smaller, while forgiveness forces you to grow beyond what you were."
                                        —*Cheri Carter-Scott*

"I define connection as the energy that exists between people when they feel seen, heard, and valued; when they can give and receive without judgment; and when they derive sustenance and strength from the relationship."
                                        —*Brene Brown*

"Your time is limited, so don't waste it living someone else's life. Don't be trapped by dogma – which is living with the results of other people's thinking. Don't let the noise of others' opinion drown out your own inner voice. And most importantly, have the courage to follow your heart and intuition."
                                        —*Steve Jobs*

"Love life, engage in it, give it all you've got. Love it with a passion, because life truly does give back, many times over, what you put into it."
                                        —*Maya Angelou*

"Knowing others is wisdom, knowing yourself is enlightenment."
                                        —*Lao Tzu*

Some of Joan's Favorite Quotes

"Life is not about waiting for the storm to pass … it's about learning to dance in the rain."

—*Vivian Greene*

"Every single thing you do matters. You have been created as one of a kind. You have been created in order to make a difference. You have within you the power to change the world."

—*Andy Andrews*

"God is preparing you for greater things. He's going to take you further than you thought possible, so don't be surprised when He asks you to think better of yourself and to act accordingly."

—*Joel Osteen*

"Embrace your essential purpose. Celebrate your best self."

—*Matthew Kelly*

"I expect to spend the rest of my life in the future, so I want to be reasonably sure of what kind of future it's going to be. That is my reason for planning."

—*Charles Kettering*

"A professional is someone who cares about the results, not just the activity. The only catch is that it takes a certain kind of person."

—*Michael Hammer, Author, Reengineering the Corporation*

"So often time it happens, we all live our life in chains, and we never even know we have the key."

—*The Eagles, "Already Gone"*

"Happiness is an attitude. We either make ourselves miserable, or happy and strong. The amount of work is the same."

—*Francesca Reigler*

"Success is living up to your potential. Don't just show up for life—live it, enjoy it, taste it, smell it and feel it."

—Joe Knapp

"When you have come to the edge of all light that you know and are about to drop off into the darkness of the unknown, faith is knowing one of two things will happen. There will be something solid to stand on or you will be taught how to fly."

—Patrick Overton

"I am brave, for God's power is greater than any situation I could possibly face today. I am not afraid, God is with me and together we are invincible."

—Unknown

Resources

Resources Joan Loves!

Good Reading

The Principle of the Path by Andy Stanley

The Rhythm of Life by Matthew Kelly

The Purpose Driven Life by Rick Warren

The Me I want to Be by John Ortberg

The Courage to Fail by Art Mortell

Even Eagles Need a Push by David McNally

Slowing Down to the Speed of Life: How to Create a More Peaceful, Simpler Life from the Inside Out by Richard Carlson and Joseph Bailey

Empowering Women: Every Woman's Guide to Successful Living by Louise L. Hay

Mission Success by Og Mandino

The Choice by Og Mandino

A Better Way to Live by Og Mandino

Your Best Life Now by Joel Osteen

It's Your Time by Joel Osteen

Success magazine

Experience Life magazine

USA Today

Experts/Inspirers/Educators

Maya Angelou

Darren Hardy

Louise Haye

Og Mandino

Joel Osteen

Dr. George Pransky

Dave Ramsey

Brian Tracy

Dr. Robert Schuller

Marianne Williamson

Women who Live a BIG Life ...

Plan

Write in Their Gratitude Journal

Keep a To-Do List

Say Affirmations

Go to the Gym

Are Organized

And Write in Their BIG Girl Diary!

Shop at www.JoanBurgeBIGLife.com

CPSIA information can be obtained
at www.ICGtesting.com
Printed in the USA
LVHW030027200419
614906LV00002B/2/P